The Best
of Spanish
Cooking

JANET MENDEL

SANTANA BOOKS

ABOUT THE AUTHOR

American journalist Janet Mendel lives in southern Spain, and has been writing about Spanish food for more than 20 years, contributing regularly to *Lookout,* Spain's magazine in English. Her previous book, *Cooking in Spain,* is considered a classic, and was described by *Taste* magazine, Great Britain, as "a brilliant guide to traditional Spanish cooking."

Janet Mendel says her interest in Spanish cuisine began early on, when she discovered that the pursuit of recipes gained her entrance into Spanish hearts, homes and kitchens.

*"**Dios también anda entre los pucheros**
(God also walks amongst the cooking pots)"*

—Saint Teresa of Avila

First published by Lookout Publications S.A. (1991)

1992 - Mirador Publications S.L., Puebla Lucía, 29640 Fuengirola
(Málaga) Spain.

1996 - Ediciones Santana S.L., Apartado 422, 29640 Fuengirola
(Málaga) Spain.

Printed by Gráficas San Pancracio, S.L.
Polg. Ind. San Luis, C/. Orotava, 17, Málaga

ISBN: 84-921229-5-1   Depósito Legal: MA-363/1996

CONTENTS

INTRODUCTION

SPAIN IS AN ENORMOUS country, offering great diversity in landscape, culture and character from south to north, east to west, coast to coast. *La cocina española,* the cuisine of Spain, reflects that diversity.

For instance, 800 years of Moorish rule in southern Spain left a culinary legacy in Andalusia of refined, almost oriental flavours; an opulent use of spices and herbs; oranges and other fruits in savoury dishes; almonds and cinnamon with meat; honeyed sweets.

The far north of Spain, a lush region of gentle rains and good pastureland, features sturdy dishes of beans, sausages and vegetables as well as some of Spain's best seafood. Unlike the rest of Spain, dairy products are widely used in cooking and some of the country's best cheeses are made in the north. The cuisines show similarities to those of neighbouring France.

The east coast of Spain, facing Italy, runs from the French border through Barcelona south to Alicante, encompassing the regions of Catalonia and the Levant. Spain probably got its pasta from Italy (pasta dishes are naturalized in Catalonia), but Italy certainly got its risottos from Valencia. Homeland of the paella, Spain's best-known dish, this region has been growing rice since the Moors introduced its cultivation, along with a complex irrigation system, many centuries ago.

The interior of Spain — the immense regions of Castile, Extremadura, La Mancha and Aragón, where great herds of sheep still move on ancient migration routes from summer to winter — is famous for its roasts: baby lamb and suckling pig done to a turn in wood-fired brick ovens. Wheat fields alternate with undulating hills tufted with olive trees; bread and oil are basic to life here. Steep ravines and dry riverbeds shelter small game — partridge and rabbit, prepared in many ways in these regions.

With thousands of miles of coastline, Spain is renowned for its fresh seafood. And it's said that one of the best fishermen's wharves in the country is in Madrid, located right in the centre of Spain! Pristine fresh fish and shellfish arriving at Mediterranean and Atlantic ports are packed on ice and shipped overnight to the capital.

Because seafood is so appreciated everywhere in Spain, a Spanish cookbook could double as a primer on fish cookery. Recipes range from simple grilled fish, often served with inspired sauces, to the fried fish so popular in the south of Spain, to the sophisticated casserole dishes of the Basques and Catalans, to myriad variations of fish soups and stews. Fish and shellfish play an important role in paella, often keeping company with such unlikely companions as chicken, pork, rabbit, and sausage, all combined in the flavourful, golden rice.

In spite of the diversity of the cuisine, several dishes appear everywhere in Spain. One is the *tortilla,* a round, flat omelette made with chopped potatoes. This is favourite fare in *tapa* bars, where a huge variety of dishes are served as appetizers with wine, sherry and beer. Another is the *cocido,* a meal-in-a-pot with garbanzos, vegetables, meat, poultry and sausages, typical home-cooked food, as is *sopa de ajo,* garlic soup, which, though it varies from one region to another, basically consists of little more than bread, oil, garlic and water. Of solid, peasant origin, the soup is better than the sum of its parts. As is that other simple soup, gazpacho, a nutritious and delicious concoction of fresh tomatoes, peppers, cucumber, and garlic, served cold in the summertime. Though originated in Andalusia, gazpacho can be found in many corners of the country. Gazpacho and paella are probably Spain's best-known dishes abroad because they're so easy to adapt to meal styles anywhere.

Spanish cooking is emphatically home cooking, based on produce indigenous to each region and prepared to traditional recipes passed down through the generations. However, some of the best of Spanish cooking today is being created fresh by the country's innovative restaurant chefs.

They take inspiration from the traditional dishes and ring changes on them. Why not pair an olive oil sauce and a butter-based hollandaise for a succulent grilled fish? Or add scraps of truffle to an old-fashioned lamb stew? Play off the richness of foie gras — Spanish-produced of course — with the sweetness of home-grown figs and tart sherry vinegar? Top an inky-black sauce with a white, grilled squid; turn that perennial Basque favourite, tiny elvers, into a salad; serve rich squares of Spanish custard atop an intense raspberry purée or freeze that old favourite, Catalan cream, into an ice; confect a sauce for grilled fish of pink sea urchin roe and a few spikes of seaweed; turn typical broad beans and ham into a salad? Some of it is whimsical and fun, some approaches high art. If these are not the *típico* dishes of the Spanish pueblo, they do make dining out in this magnificent country an exhilarating experience.

If you are travelling in Spain, be adventuresome and seek out the regional culinary specialities and also try the *nueva cocina,* Spain's version of *nouvelle cuisine.* Either way, you'll enjoy some fine eating. Spanish cuisine "travels well" and is not difficult to re-create in other climes.

When you get back home, try some of the best of Spanish cooking in your own kitchen. You'll find lots of useful information about ingredients, substitutions and adaptations in the glossary at the back of the book, in the chapter on "Gastronomic Souvenirs" and, of course, in the recipes.

WINE AND TAPAS

NOT SIMPLY A PLACE to drink, nor just an eatery, a Spanish *tapa* bar is where you meet your friends for a glass of wine, some titbits of good food and plenty of lively conversation. The best *tapa* bars in Spain tend to be crowded, a bit brash and noisy, and really friendly.

Tapas, tiny portions of food, are one of the best introductions to Spanish cooking.

They say that Spaniards like to eat standing up. The locals can put away what amounts to a whole meal while just standing at the bar, sipping dry sherry, and having an animated conversation with friends. Later they will go on to eat a full meal!

Tapas may be simple: fat, herb-scented olives, toasted almonds, hard-boiled quails' eggs, paper-thin slices of *serrano* ham, sliced sausages, aged cheese, prawns in their shells. Then come *tapas de cocina,* those from the kitchen, such as fried foods: croquettes, batter-dipped prawns, ham rolls stuffed with cheese, bite-sized pieces of crisp-fried fish, vegetable fritters. And salads: *pipirrana,* a tomato-onion-pepper relish; *campera,* sliced potatoes, onions and olives in a lemony dressing; *remojón,* an exotic combination of oranges, onions and cod; *pulpo,* diced octopus with tomatoes, garlic and parsley; roasted peppers.

Seafood selections might include *gambas al pil pil,* prawns sizzled with garlic; clams or mussels *a la marinera; cazón en adobo,* tangy, marinated fried fish; *boquerones al natural,* fresh anchovies dressed with garlic and vinegar. Shellfish, *mariscos,* in impressive variety, hold pride of place at any tapa bar. Generally they are simply prepared, boiled in sea water — prawns large and small, clams, mussels, oysters, scallops, crabs of many sizes and hues, lobster with and without claws, whelks, and even barnacles, *percebes,* a delectable sea titbit made almost as pricey as caviare for the difficulty of its gathering on sheer rock cliffs off the Galician coast.

Meatballs, rabbit in almond sauce, chicken with garlic, tiny pork cutlets, stewed tripe with garbanzos, kidneys in sherry sauce, spicy Moroccan-style kebabs, lamb stew, sautéd mushrooms, and, of course, *tortilla,* thick potato omelette.

Olives are on their home ground here. (No, you can't eat them straight from the tree; they are impossibly bitter and must first be cured.) Try country-style olives, slightly bitter and redolent of thyme, fennel, garlic and lemon.

Try, too, the much-appreciated Spanish ham, *jamón serrano,* called "mountain" hams because they're usually made in cool, dry mountain regions. Salt-cured and aged from seven months to several years, they are served raw as an aperitif. The colour is deep red to scarlet and the texture is chewy and more or less dry, depending on age. The most appreciated hams are those with surnames, such as *de Jabugo* (Huelva), *de Pedroches* (Córdoba), *de Teruel* and *de Trevélez* (Granada) and, in particular, those made of *pata negra,* black-footed, brown Iberian pigs, which roam semi-wild and feed on acorns. Their flesh is incredibly sweet. These hams are very expensive.

Other noble contributions from the pig are various sausages such as *chorizo,* spicy with garlic and paprika; *lomo adobado,* cured pork loin; smoky *longaniza,* and *salchichón,* pepper-studded hard sausage.

Spanish cheeses nicely accompany aperitif wines. Best known is Manchego, traditionally produced in the central region of La Mancha, of ewes' milk. Well-aged, it is splintery, mellow, but with a satisfying "bite."

Some tapa bars specialize in just a few selections, others may have as many as 40 different dishes. A tapa really is just a nibble — in some bars, served free with wine. For a larger serving, ask for a *ración.*

Tapas are wonderfully adaptable to modern entertaining, providing a tantalizing array of foods which easily suit a sophisticated cocktail party or an informal buffet. You could put together a party menu from the above listings and the recipes which follow. Many other recipes in this book are typically served as tapas, simply by cutting portions into bite-size bits. Similarly, many tapa dishes become starters, salads, side dishes or main attractions by changing the serving proportions.

Tapas were invented in the south, in Andalusia. This is

storybook Spain — flamenco flounces and gypsy bullfighters; heady, jasmine-scented patios and the sound of fountains and guitars in the twilight; olive trees, and glittering, golden beaches.

Andalusia is where two of the world's finest aperitif wines — sherry and its close cousin, Montilla-Moriles — are made. Both have an alcohol content considerably higher than table wines. So, you see why food is essential!

The dry ones — *fino, manzanilla* and *amontillado* — vary from the colour of pale straw to topaz; their flavour is nutty without a trace of sweetness. Richer on the palate are the *olorosos* and *palos cortados,* gold in colour and velvety in texture, also appreciated as aperitifs. Sweet and cream sherries range from amber to mahogany and are good with biscuits for afternoon tea or with coffee and pastries after a meal.

Both sherry and Montilla are made by the *solera* system of blending and ageing. In the bodegas (wineries) barrels are stacked several deep. New wines are added to the top ones. As mature wine is drawn off from the bottom casks for bottling, each successive barrel is topped up from the one above.

Don't be afraid to try sherry, in Spain or at home. There's nothing fuddy-duddy about this wine. It's crisp and clean and full of warmth. Dry sherry has a flavour quotient as high as fine whisky — but you can drink a lot more sherry than whisky before feeling the effects. In a tapa bar, just ask for a *fino* (pronounced "feeno"). The mellow and sweet ones easily fill that after-dinner craving for slow sipping, without the cloying sweetness of many liqueurs. Málaga muscatel wine, sometimes called "liquid raisin," also is delicious with fruit and pastries.

Spain also produces superb table wines, red *(tinto),* white *(blanco)* and rosé *(rosado).* You will find an excellent selection of them at your local wine merchant, for Spanish wines are widely exported — and at very good prices.

The important information on a Spanish wine label is the *Denominación de Origen* (D.O.), or designation of origin. To qualify for D.O., the winery must meet standards set by the region's committee. As you get to know Spanish wines, you will soon be choosing your favourite bodegas, equivalent to France's *chateau* designation.

The best table wines come from Rioja, Penedés and Ribera del Duero. Valdepeñas and La Mancha produce huge quantities of very palatable, less expensive wines, perfect for everyday imbibing or making *sangría*, fruity wine punch. Almost all Spanish table wines, including the finest, are made from several blended grape varieties.

Wine labels tell you the year of the harvest *(cosecha)* and the length of time the wine was aged. A wine bottled in the first year carries a *garantía de origen* label; an aged wine is *de crianza,* and exceptional aged wines are *reserva* or *gran reserva.* The length of time the wine is aged varies by region. For example, Rioja *crianza* wines must be aged one year in oak and one year in the bottle.

A restaurant's *vino de la casa,* house wine, is generally good value for money.

Cava is the name in Spain for sparkling wines made according to the "champagne" method. Spanish bubbly comes from the Catalan region of Penedés. Serious competition to French champagne, cava adds glitter to any occasion.

ACEITUNAS
Olives

Spanish olives are famous the world over. But in Spain they are special, often home-cured with herbs, garlic and lemon. Rinse bottled or tinned, unstuffed green olives and place in a glass jar. Add thyme, fennel, slivers of garlic, thin wedges of lemon. Sprinkle with salt and add water to cover. Top with olive oil and let the olives marinate for a week before serving.

TORTILLITAS DE CAMARONES
Prawn Fritters

1/2	onion
2tbsp	parsley
250g | 9oz	peeled prawns
250g | 9oz	flour
1/4tsp	baking powder
1/4litre | 1/2pt	water
3tbsp	white wine
1tsp	salt
	oil for frying

Mince the onion and parsley in blender or processor. Add the peeled prawns, flour, baking powder, water, wine and salt. Process briefly to mince prawns and blend flour. Let the batter rest for 3 hours. Heat enough oil to cover bottom of a frying pan and drop spoonfuls of batter into the oil. Fry until browned and turn, like a pancake, to brown the other side. Remove and drain on paper towelling. Serve hot. Makes about 3 dozen.

GAMBAS EN GABARDINA
Prawns in Anoraks

300g | 10oz	peeled prawns
	toothpicks
1	egg
3tbsp	water
1/2tsp	salt
1/2tsp	baking powder
75g | 2 1/2oz	flour
	oil for deep frying

Spear each prawn on a toothpick and set aside. Beat the egg with the water. Add the salt and baking powder and beat in the flour, making a thick batter. Let it sit for an hour. Heat oil in a deep fryer. Dip the prawns — toothpicks and all — into the batter and fry them until golden. Serve piping hot with lemon and *salsa brava* — "fierce" sauce.

Salsa brava: blend 4 tablespoons mayonnaise, 8 tablespoons ketchup, 2 tablespoons vinegar, 1 teaspoon paprika, 1/2 teaspoon ground cumin and enough cayenne to pack a punch.

PAPANDUAS
Fritters

Use this batter for any bits of cooked fish, meat or vegetables. Typically, these fritters are made with *bacalao,* salt cod, soaked overnight, lightly cooked and de-boned.

1/2	small onion
1	clove garlic
1tbsp	parsley
1/4tsp	crumbled saffron
150g | 5oz	flour
1/2tsp	baking powder
1/2tsp	salt
1	egg, separated
150ml | 1/4pt	water, approximately
300g | 10oz	cooked fish, sausage, meat or vegetables
	oil for frying

If using salt cod, soak it overnight in water to cover, changing the water at least once. Simmer it in fresh water to cover for 5 minutes, then drain. Remove all skin and bones and cut in pieces. If using chorizo or other sausage, cut into small chunks, removing casing. In blender or processor mince the onion, garlic and parsley. Add saffron, flour, baking powder, salt, egg yolk and water, and blend until smooth. Let the batter sit for an hour. Whip the egg whites until stiff and fold into the batter. Dip the pieces of food into the batter and fry in deep, hot oil until crisp and golden. Drain and serve hot.

Tip: Use this batter for slices of aubergine, salted and patted dry; cooked artichoke hearts, cut in quarters.

FLAMENQUINES
Ham Rolls

Top slices of cooked ham with thinly sliced cheese. A piece of pickle or red pimento in the centre makes for extra interest. Roll up the ham and cheese. Dredge the rolls in flour, dip them in beaten egg, then roll in fine breadcrumbs. Set them aside to dry for 20 minutes. Fry in hot oil until golden on all sides. Drain on absorbent paper and serve hot.

CROQUETAS
Croquettes

3tbsp	butter or oil
1tbsp	minced onion
55g | 2oz	flour
225m | 8fl oz	milk
1tsp	salt
	grating of nutmeg
1	egg yolk
100g | 3 1/2oz	minced ham, tuna, or other cooked meat or fish
	beaten egg
	fine breadcrumbs
	oil for frying

Melt the butter in a saucepan and soften the minced onion in it. Stir in the flour and cook for 2 minutes. Then whisk in the milk and cook on a low heat, stirring constantly, until the sauce is very thick. Season with salt and nutmeg. Whisk in the egg yolk and the minced ham or other filling. Spread the mixture on a plate and chill it for at least 3 hours. Scoop up small balls of the mixture and shape them into round or oblong croquettes. Dredge them in flour, dip in beaten egg and roll in breadcrumbs. Set them aside to dry for 20 minutes, then fry in deep, hot oil until golden and crisp. Drain on absorbent paper and serve immediately.

EMPANADILLAS
Pork Pasties

Canapés with pizazz. Vary the filling, using tuna, chicken, prawns, or ham, finely chopped, instead of the pork.

For the dough:

275g | 9 1/2oz	flour
100g | 3 1/2oz	butter or lard
1/2tsp	salt
100m | 3 1/2fl oz	water or wine

Place the flour in a bowl and add chilled butter or lard, cutting it in with a knife until the mixture is crumbly. Add salt and then the liquid. Mix into a ball and knead very briefly on a floured board. Cover with plastic wrap and chill for at least 2 hours.

For the filling:

200g | 7oz	minced pork
2tbsp	oil
2tbsp	minced onion
1	clove minced garlic
3tbsp	tomato sauce
1tbsp	chopped parsley
1/4tsp	crushed oregano
1tbsp	brandy or sherry
50g | 2oz	pitted or stuffed olives, chopped
1	egg, beaten
	salt and pepper

Fry the minced pork in the oil until browned. Add the minced onion and garlic. Then stir in the tomato sauce, parsley, oregano, brandy and chopped olives. Simmer this mixture until the liquid is reduced. Stir in the beaten egg and season with salt and pepper.

Roll out the pastry dough on a floured board and cut into circles of about 10cm I 4in. Place a teaspoonful of filling on each pastry round and fold the dough over to make a half-moon. Crimp the edges with the tines of a fork. Fry the pasties, a few at a time, in deep, hot oil until golden, or bake in a preheated hot oven. Makes about 2 dozen.

BOLLOS PREÑADOS
Stuffed Buns

Another fine canapé. Roll out thawed, frozen puff pastry. Cut into rounds. Lay a piece of chorizo sausage on each and top with another pastry round. Brush the pastry with egg beaten with a little milk and bake in a preheated hot oven until the pastry is browned. You could also use pie-crust dough.

GAMBAS A LA PLANCHA
Grilled Prawns

In Spain prawns are often served without adornment, without a sauce, a real treat when they are wonderfully fresh. In any case, a garlic mayonnaise *(alioli)* or red pepper sauce *(romesco)* are excellent accompaniments.

Choose large prawns, either *gambas* or *langostinos.* Wash them, drain well and pat dry. Leave them whole and unshelled. Brush a griddle with a little oil and heat it very hot. Sprinkle with coarse salt and lay the whole prawns on the griddle. Cook them on one side until they turn pink, about 3 minutes. Using tongs, turn them to cook reverse side for another 3 minutes.

Variation: PARRILLADA DE PESCADOS Y MARISCOS, Mixed Seafood Grill. Grill slices of angler and hake, mussels, clams, lobster, etc. with the prawns on a hot griddle.

ALIOLI
Garlic Mayonnaise

1	egg
4	cloves garlic
175ml | 6fl oz	olive oil
2tbsp	vinegar or lemon juice
1/2tsp	salt

In a blender place the egg and peeled garlic. Whirl until garlic is smooth. Add the oil in a slow stream, with the motor running, until the sauce is thick and emulsified. Add the vinegar or lemon juice and salt.

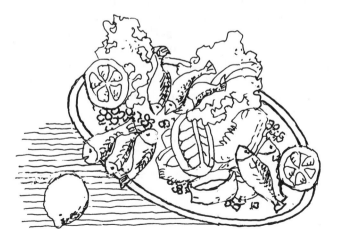

ROMESCO
Catalan Pepper Sauce

Sensational with roast chicken, grilled prawns, lobster, sautéd or poached fish, veggies, salad greens, jacket potatoes. It is best made with dried, sweet red peppers. Otherwise substitute strong paprika.

50g | 2oz	dried red peppers *(ñoras)*
1/4litre | 1/2pt	olive oil
2	dozen skinned almonds and/or hazelnuts
3	cloves garlic, peeled
1	slice bread (30g | 1oz)
	cayenne or chilli to taste
1/2tsp	salt
1/4tsp	pepper
2tbsp	brandy
2tbsp	vinegar
1tbsp	tomato sauce

Put the peppers in water to cover and bring to the boil. Simmer for 5 minutes, remove from heat and let them soak for 20 minutes. Heat 4 tablespoons of the oil in a heavy pan and in it fry the nuts and garlic until lightly golden. Skim out and reserve. Fry the slice of bread in the same oil until crisp. (If sauce is for salad greens, omit the bread for a thinner consistency.) Let the oil cool. Split open the peppers, discarding seeds and stems. Scrape the pulp from the skins. You should have about 2 tablespoons of pulp. Place in a processor, blender or mortar with the toasted nuts, garlic, bread, cayenne, salt and pepper and process until smooth. Add the brandy, vinegar, tomato sauce, then the remaining olive oil. Serve the sauce at room temperature or add it to a sauté dish at the very end of cooking time. Thin as necessary with fish or meat stock.

GAMBAS AL PIL PIL
Sizzling Prawns

For one serving:

3	tablespoons olive oil
1	clove garlic, chopped
	pinch minced chilli pepper

pinch paprika
10   peeled prawns

Use earthenware or other heat-proof ramekins for individual servings. Place in each small casserole, the oil, chopped garlic, chilli pepper, paprika and prawns. Place on to direct heat or in a very hot pre-heated oven until the oil is sizzling and the prawns are just pink and curled. Serve immediately, while the oil is still *pil-pileando,* with chunks of bread for dipping into the sauce.

ALMEJAS A LA MARINERA
Fisherman's Clams

1kg | 2lb	clams, well scrubbed
4tbsp	olive oil
4	cloves garlic, chopped
50ml | 2fl oz	white wine
50ml | 2fl oz	water
2tbsp	fine breadcrumbs
	freshly ground pepper
2tbsp	chopped parsley

Put the oil, chopped garlic, wine and water into a pot big enough to hold the clams. Bring it to the boil and add the clams. Cover the pot and shake it until the shells open. Sprinkle in the breadcrumbs, pepper and chopped parsley and cook for another minute. Serve the clams and their broth in soup bowls.

Tip: Mussels can be prepared in the same manner. Fresh tomatoes, peeled and chopped, and a little minced onion can be added to the pot before the clams or mussels.

CALAMARES FRITOS
Fried Squid Rings

If it weren't for the fact that this Spanish speciality looks a lot like deep-fried onion rings, visitors would probably never touch them. What happens is that, once innocently sampled in a tapa bar, they become addictive... and are ever so easy to prepare at home, with either fresh or frozen squid.

Unlike the octopus or cuttlefish, the squid is fairly tender and quick-cooking, if it's not too big — meaning under 450g | 1lb. Its body is a slender pouch from which protrudes a head with short tentacles. Grasp the head and pull gently. It will come away from the body pouch bringing the innards with it. Still inside is the cartilage, which looks like a strip of transparent plastic. Grasp the top of it and pull it out. Rinse the pouch and pull off the membrane on the outside. The wing flaps will come off too. Save them. Now, cut off the tentacles just above the eyes. Save the tentacles and discard the remaining head and innards. (Save the ink sac if you need it for sauce. The ink is enclosed in a silvery pouch on the innards. Cut it free without breaking.) With scissors, cut the body pouch crosswise into rings. The wing flaps and tentacles can be left whole or cut in half.

Once washed and dried, dredge the pieces of prepared squid in flour, then shake in a sieve to remove excess flour. Fry in deep, hot olive oil until they are golden and crisp. Remove, sprinkle with salt and serve hot with lemon wedges.

PULPO A LA FEIRIA
Octopus Titbits

1 1/2kg	3 1/2lb	octopus, cleaned (about 800g | 2lb cleaned and frozen)
1kg	2lb	potatoes
6	cloves garlic, minced
3tsp	paprika
	pinch of cayenne
150ml	1/4pt	olive oil
1tsp	coarse salt

Pound octopus with a mallet to tenderize it. Blanch in boiling water, rinse and drain well. (It can be frozen at this point and cooked later, a process which helps to tenderize it.) Put to cook in salted water and simmer until tender, about 2 hours (pressure cooker reduces cooking time). With scissors, cut the octopus into small squares, discarding the stomach and beak. Separately, cook the potatoes until tender. Peel them and cut in pieces. Arrange octopus and potato pieces on wooden plates. Mix the minced garlic, paprika, cayenne and oil. Sprinkle the octopus and potatoes with salt and drizzle with the oil mixture.

BOQUERONES AL NATURAL
Marinated Fresh Anchovies

This tapa bar favourite is made with tiny, fresh anchovies. If not available, fresh sardines or herring, cut in thin strips, might be substituted.

1/2kg | 1lb	fresh anchovies *(boquerones)*
1/4litre | 1/2pt	wine vinegar
1tsp	salt
50ml | 2fl oz	olive oil
4	cloves garlic, minced
2tbsp	chopped parsley

Cut off heads, gut the fish and remove backbones. (Grasp top of spine and pull down sharply, leaving the two fillets attached at the tail.) Wash and place the fillets in a single layer in a glass or enamelled dish. Add enough vinegar to cover them and add the salt. Marinate from 8 to 24 hours, or until the fillets are white and solid. Drain them, rinse in iced water and arrange on a bed of shredded lettuce. Mix the olive oil, minced garlic and chopped parsley and drizzle over the fish. Garnish with sliced lemon and onion rings.

CAZON EN ADOBO
Fried Marinated Fish

Cazón, dogfish, is one of several edible sharks now widely marketed. The marinade compensates for blandness of flavour and can be used with any fish of solid texture.

3/4kg | 1 3/4lb	dogfish or similar
50ml | 2fl oz	olive oil
50ml | 2fl oz	wine vinegar or lemon juice
1tbsp	water
3	cloves garlic, minced
1/4tsp	paprika
1tsp	oregano
1/4tsp	ground pepper
	pinch of cumin
1/2tsp	salt
	flour
	oil for frying

Cut the fish into cubes, discarding skin and bone. Put it in a glass or ceramic bowl. Mix together the oil, vinegar, water, chopped garlic, paprika, oregano, pepper, cumin and salt. Pour over the fish and mix well. Marinate for at least 6 hours or overnight. Drain the fish, dredge it in flour and fry in hot oil until golden and crisp. Serve very hot, sprinkled with salt.

TORTILLA ESPAÑOLA
Spanish Omelette

Americans, when they hear the word *"tortilla,"* think of Mexican flat cornmeal bread. And the English, when they hear "omelette" expect the French sort, folded over a filling of cheese or ham. The Spanish omelette is neither one nor the other. It's round — thus a *torta* — and an omelette, thus the eggs. The classic potato omelette is round and thick like a pie. Serve it cut into squares for tapas or into wedges, for picnics, breakfast, lunch or supper.

1kg | 2lb	potatoes
3tbsp	chopped onions
50ml | 2fl oz	olive oil

| 4-5 | eggs, beaten to combine |
| 1/2tsp | salt |

A treated, non-stick frying pan works well for this omelette. Peel the potatoes and cut them in dice or slice thinly with a processor. Heat the oil in a frying pan (20cm I 8in diameter) and add the potatoes and chopped onions. Fry them very slowly until tender, turning frequently, without letting them brown. Drain off the oil, reserving it, and place the potatoes in a bowl. Stir the beaten eggs into the potato mixture and add salt. Return the oil to the fryng pan, adding a little more if necessary. Pour in the potato-egg mixture and cook on a medium heat until the omelette is set on the bottom, shaking the pan to keep the omelette from sticking as it cooks. It should be golden, not deeply browned. Place a plate or flat lid over the pan and reverse the omelette on to it. Slide it back into the pan, uncooked side down, and cook until the bottom is set and just slightly browned.

Variation: TORTILLA CAPUCHINA. Reduce the chopped potatoes by half and add 100g I 3 1/2oz cooked asparagus tips and 1 tablespoon chopped parsley. Cook in the same manner as above.

HUEVOS RELLENOS
Stuffed Eggs

8	eggs
200g I 7oz	cooked prawns
8	green olives, chopped
1	tinned pimento
1tsp	lemon juice
	salt and pepper
100ml I 3 1/2fl oz	mayonnaise

Hard cook the eggs for 5 minutes. Rinse them in cold water, then shell them. Cut the eggs in half lengthwise. Remove the yolks and reserve the whites. Chop the prawns and mix them in a small bowl with the chopped olives, half of the pimento, finely chopped, the salt and pepper and lemon juice. Fill the egg whites with this mixture. Arrange them on lettuce leaves. Top each egg with mayonnaise and a strip of pimento. Sieve the egg yolks and sprinkle over the eggs.

ENSALADA CAMPERA
Country Potato Salad

1kg | 2lb	potatoes
1	small onion
1	large tomato, peeled and chopped
1	lemon
50ml | 2fl oz	olive oil
2tbsp	chopped parsley
100ml | 3 1/2fl oz	mayonnaise
2	hard-cooked eggs, sliced
1	small tin pimentos
12	pitted olives
1	small tin tuna

Cook potatoes in their skins in water until tender. Drain well, peel and slice them into a bowl. Add the chopped onion and tomato to the potatoes. Add the juice of a large lemon, the olive oil, chopped parsley, mayonnaise, sliced eggs, chopped pimentos and pitted olives. Toss lightly. Garnish with chunks of tuna. Serves 4-6.

REMOJON
Orange and Cod Salad

200g | 7oz	dry salt cod (or 1 tin tuna)
1	onion, thinly sliced
3-4	oranges
1	clove garlic, crushed
3tbsp	olive oil
1tbsp	vinegar
	chilli pepper (optional)
50g | 2oz	pitted olives

Toast the salt cod over a flame or under the grill, until it is lightly browned and softened. Put in a bowl of water for a few hours, changing the water once. In a bowl, combine the thinly sliced onion with the oranges, peeled, seeded and thinly sliced or chopped. Whisk the crushed garlic with the olive oil, vinegar and finely minced chilli. Drain the cod and remove all skin and bones. Shred it and add to the salad (or substitute tinned tuna). Toss with the dressing and place in a serving bowl. Let marinate, chilled, for several hours. Garnish with olives, preferably the slightly bitter, home-cured green olives, available in Spain, or Greek or Niçoise-style black olives.

ENSALADA DE ZANAHORIAS
Carrot Salad

1kg | 2lb	carrots
3tbsp	seeded raisins
1tbsp	pine-nuts
2tbsp	chopped onion
2tbsp	chopped parsley
2	cloves garlic, minced
8tbsp	olive oil
4tbsp	wine vinegar
	juice of 1 lemon
	salt and pepper

Peel the carrots and cut in thin slices or matchsticks. Cook in salted water to cover until crisp-tender. Drain and rinse in cold water. Place the carrots in a bowl and add the seeded raisins, pine-nuts, chopped onion and chopped parsley. In a small bowl, mix the minced garlic, olive oil, vinegar and salt and pepper. Add to the salad and toss lightly. Marinate for several hours before serving. Garnish with a few leaves of fresh herbs — mint, tarragon, thyme. Serves 6.

CHAMPIÑONES AL AJILLO
Garlic-Sizzled Mushrooms

1/2kg | 1lb	mushrooms
100ml | 3 1/2fl oz	olive oil
1	head garlic (about 10 cloves)
1	chilli pepper (optional)
1/2tsp	salt
	freshly ground pepper
2tbsp	parsley

Clean the mushrooms. Slice them if large or quarter if small. Heat the oil in a frying pan or earthenware casserole and sauté the mushrooms with the chopped cloves of garlic and chilli pepper. Cook about 10 minutes and season with salt and pepper. Sprinkle with chopped parsley. Substitute wild mushrooms such as *cepes* or *chanterelles*.

Variation: CHAMPIÑONES RELLENOS, Stuffed Mushrooms. Stuff mushroom caps with minced ham, onion, garlic and breadcrumbs, sautéd together. Bake or gently sauté them as in the above recipe.

ALBONDIGAS
Meatballs

1/2kg | 1lb	minced pork and/or veal
2	slices bread (50g | 2oz)
1	clove garlic, minced
2tbsp	finely chopped onion
2tbsp	chopped parsley
1/2tsp	salt
1/4tsp	ground pepper
	freshly grated nutmeg
1	egg, beaten
	flour
	oil

Almond Sauce:

25	almonds, blanched and skinned
1	slice bread (25g | 1oz.)
2	cloves garlic
3tbsp	olive oil
10	peppercorns
1/2tsp	saffron
1	clove
1/2tsp	salt
100ml | 3 1/2fl oz	white wine
1/4litre | 1/2pt	meat stock or water

Place the minced meat in a bowl. Soak the sliced bread in water or milk to cover until softened. Squeeze out and add to the meat with the minced garlic, chopped onion, chopped parsley, salt, pepper, nutmeg and beaten egg. Knead well to make a smooth mixture. Form into small balls. Roll them in flour and fry slowly in hot oil until browned on all sides. Remove. Make the almond sauce. Fry the blanched almonds, bread and garlic in the oil until toasted. Remove. In a mortar or blender, crush the peppercorns, saffron, clove and salt with the toasted almonds, bread and garlic. Add the wine to make a smooth paste. Add to the oil remaining in the pan, then add the stock or water. Cook for a few minutes, then add the fried meatballs. Simmer the meatballs for 25 minutes, adding additional liquid if needed. Immediately before serving, add a squeeze of lemon juice and a sprinkling of parsley.

Tip: Alternatively, finish the meatballs in a fresh tomato or sherry sauce. Use this meatball mixture to stuff peppers, aubergines or courgettes.

PINCHOS MORUNOS
Moroccan Style Kebabs

Served as tapas or party snacks, these kebabs are usually cooked over charcoal braziers. The meat is cut into tiny cubes and served with chunks of bread. In Morocco, of course, the meat would be lamb, but in Spain it is as likely to be pork or veal. The spices can be purchased at Spanish markets — ask for *especias para pinchitos,* kebab spice. If not available, mix equal quantities of curry powder with ground cumin.

1kg | 2lb	pork, lamb or beef
4tbsp	chopped parsley
10	cloves garlic, chopped
2	large lemons, juiced
1tbsp	pinchito spice
1/2tsp	cayenne or red pepper flakes (optional)
1tsp	salt

Cut the meat into small cubes. In a glass or crockery bowl layer it with chopped parsley, chopped garlic, lemon juice, spices and salt. Marinate, refrigerated, for 8 to 24 hours, turning the mixture several times. Thread 4 or 5 pieces of the meat on thin, metal skewers and grill over charcoal or under grill until browned on all sides. Makes about 20 kebabs. Serve with bread cut in chunks.

CHORIZO AL INFIERNO
Sausage With Anise Brandy

Chorizo is a typical Spanish sausage well-flavoured with garlic and paprika. Hard varieties are simply sliced and served with bread. Soft ones, more like link sausage, are fried or added to stewed bean and lentil dishes.

300g | 10oz	chorizo links
3tbsp	oil
2tbsp	chopped onion
5tbsp	dry anise brandy or Pacharan

Cut the sausage links into bite-size pieces. Fry them in the oil with the chopped onion until browned. Add the anise brandy, heat it slightly, and set alight. Swirl the pan until flames subside. Serve immediately, sprinkled with chopped parsley or a little chopped fennel leaves.

PLANCHITAS
Grilled Pork Cutlets

400g | 14oz	pork cutlets
5	cloves garlic, chopped
2tbsp	chopped parsley
1	large lemon, juiced
	salt and pepper

The pork cutlets should be thinly sliced and cut into regular-sized pieces about 6 cm | 2 1/2in. Place them in a single layer on a plate. Sprinkle with the garlic, parsley, lemon juice and salt and pepper. Leave to marinate for 2 hours. Heat a griddle or a heavy frying pan and brush it lightly with oil. Cook the cutlets on the griddle turning once, until browned on both sides. Serve atop slices of bread accompanied by lemon wedges. Pork fillet can be prepared in the same manner.

RIÑONES AL JEREZ
Kidneys in Sherry Sauce

850g | 2lb	lamb or veal kidneys
4tbsp	olive oil
2tbsp	chopped onion
1	clove garlic, minced
1tbsp	flour
1	bay-leaf
1/4tsp	crumbled thyme
100ml | 3 1/2fl oz	dry sherry
100ml | 3 1/2fl oz	meat stock

salt and pepper
chopped parsley

Wash the kidneys, soak for an hour in salted water. If using pork or beef kidneys, blanch in acidulated water for 15 minutes. Remove outer membrane and cut kidneys into cubes. Heat the oil in a frying pan and sauté the kidneys on a very gentle heat, and remove. Add the chopped onion and minced garlic to the oil and sauté until softened. Stir in the flour, then add the bay-leaf, thyme, sherry, meat stock, and salt and pepper. Simmer until thickened. Add the kidneys and simmer on a very low heat for 10 minutes. Do not boil. Season with salt and pepper and serve sprinkled with chopped parsley. Makes 6-8 tapa servings.

CALLOS
Stewed Tripe

A popular tapa in Madrid bars, it is easy to prepare if you can buy ready-cooked tripe. Otherwise follow the directions for cleaning and cooking. In Andalusia, the dish often includes *garbanzos,* chick-peas, and may be made with pig tripe instead of veal.

1kg | 2lb	cooked calves' tripe
1	cooked calf's foot
75ml | 2 1/2fl oz	oil
1	onion, chopped
1	carrot, chopped
100g | 3 1/2oz	serrano ham or bacon, diced
1tbsp	flour
4	cloves garlic
1tbsp	paprika
100ml | 3 1/2fl oz	tomato sauce
1tsp	freshly ground pepper
	cayenne or chilli to taste
1/2tsp	ground cumin
	salt to taste
200g | 7oz	chorizo or longaniza sausage

To clean and prepare uncooked tripe: first wash it well under running water, scraping it with a knife to clean off bits of fat. Spread it out and sprinkle with coarse salt. Scrub with a cut lemon on both sides, adding more salt and more lemon as needed. Rinse well. With scissors, cut the tripe into squares about 4cm | 1 1/2in. Put in a bowl and sprinkle with salt and pour over it a glass of vinegar. Let it sit for an hour, turning occasionally. Rinse again. Put the tripe in a pot and cover with water. Bring to the boil, skimming off the froth, and boil 5 minutes. Drain. Put the pieces of tripe in fresh water with bay-leaf, an onion stuck with cloves, a few peppercorns and several cloves of garlic. Bring to the boil, skim, then simmer until the tripe is tender, about 3 hours. A calf's foot, skinned, split, well-scrubbed and blanched in boiling water, can be cooked with the tripe. After cooking, remove bones and cut the meat into pieces. The tripe can be prepared up to this point and refrigerated, with the broth, until the following day.

Drain the tripe, saving the broth. Put tripe in a casserole with the pieces of calf's foot. In a frying pan heat the oil and sauté the chopped onion, carrot, diced ham and garlic. Stir in the flour and the paprika, then the tomato sauce and about 1/4litre | 1/2 pint of the reserved broth. Season with pepper, cayenne, cumin and salt. Pour over the tripe and add the chorizo. Cook slowly for an hour, adding additional broth as needed. The sauce should be thick. Before serving, cut the chorizo into slices and arrange on top of the tripe. Serves 6.

DRINKS

SANGRIA
Red Wine Punch

1	bottle chilled red wine
150ml | 4fl oz	brandy or Cointreau
100g | 3 1/2oz	sugar
	sliced fruit
	soda water

In a pitcher mix the brandy or Cointreau with the sugar until dissolved. Add a variety of sliced fruit — oranges, bananas, apples, strawberries are typical — and macerate, refrigerated, until serving time. Add the chilled red wine and dilute to taste with soda water or *gaseosa,* a sweet soda water.

ZURRA
White Wine Cooler

1	bottle chilled white wine
200ml | 7fl oz	water
50g | 2oz	sugar
	sprigs of fresh mint
1	stalk celery with leaves
1	piece of cinnamon
1	sliced lemon
1	sliced orange
1	sliced peach

Boil the sugar and water until sugar is dissolved. Remove from heat and add the mint, celery, cinnamon, lemon and orange slices. Let steep until the syrup is cooled. Strain into a pitcher and add the chilled wine, the peach slices and a few slices of lemon and orange. Dilute to taste with soda water and garnish with fresh mint.

MARIA SANGRIA
Bloody Mary

Fill a tall glass or mug with ice. Pour over 30ml | 1fl oz of vodka. Fill the glass with gazpacho (see next chapter for recipe). Add a dash of Tabasco sauce and a swizzle-stick of cucumber or green pepper. Stir well.

DESTORNILLADOR
Screwdriver

Mix 1/2litre | 1pt freshly squeezed orange juice with 225ml | 8fl oz dry or medium dry sherry. Add cracked ice and stir.

SOUPS, SALADS AND STARTERS

IN SPAIN THE MAIN MEAL of the day is served at midday
— meaning between 2 and 3pm — and generally consists of at
least three courses. A soup, salad, egg or vegetable dish would
precede a main course of meat or fish, with fresh fruit or a
pudding to follow. For an "important" meal, both a seafood and
meat course might be served. Of the following starters, some
of them could also be main courses and some of the tapa dishes
in the preceding chapter could easily be starters.

SOUPS

Soups in Spain, with the exception of the cold ones of
Andalusia, are generally of the sturdy, stick-to-the-ribs
variety, including potages of lentils and other pulses and a
wonderful variety of seafood soups.

CALDO GALLEGO
Galician Soup

Grelos, a much-appreciated green in Galicia, would typically go into this hearty soup. These are turnip tops, whose slightly bitter flavour combines nicely with pork and ham. In Andalusia, a similar soup, *berza de acelga,* is made with chard. If neither is available, use chopped cabbage, kale or collards.

250g | 9oz	white beans
300g | 10oz	meaty ham bone or cured ribs
200g | 7oz	stewing beef
50g '2oz	salt pork or bacon
3litres | 5 1/4pt	water
2	bay-leaves
350g | 3/4lb	turnip greens, cabbage or chard
3	medium potatoes
	salt and pepper
2tbsp	oil
1	clove crushed garlic
1tbsp	paprika

Soak the beans overnight in water to cover. Separately, soak the ham bone or cured ribs to de-salt them. Put beans to cook in the water. When partially cooked, add the ham, beef, salt pork or bacon and bay-leaves. Simmer for an hour. Chop the greens and dice the potatoes. Add to the soup with salt and pepper and continue cooking until tender. Remove a spoonful of beans and potatoes to blender and purée them with the oil, crushed garlic and paprika. Return to the soup and cook another few minutes. Serves 6.

SOPA DE AJO
Garlic Soup

6tbsp	olive oil
4	cloves (or more) garlic
6	slices bread
1tsp	paprika
1 1/4litres | 2 1/4pt	boiling water or stock
2tsp	salt
4	eggs
	chopped parsley

Heat the oil in a soup pot or heat-proof casserole and add the chopped garlic. Remove crusts from bread and cut into cubes. Add to the oil and fry until lightly golden. Stir in the paprika and immediately add the boiling liquid. Cover and simmer for 20 minutes or until the bread is almost dissolved in the broth. Place the soup in four individual earthenware bowls and add one egg to each. Poach the eggs in the soup in the oven or on top of the cooker until whites are set. Garnish with chopped parsley.

Variation: Fry chopped onion and peeled, chopped tomato with the garlic. Sprinkle grated cheese over the egg and put in a hot oven until egg is set.

SOPA DE ALMENDRAS
Almond Soup

4tbsp	olive oil
150g | 5oz	blanched almonds
2	cloves garlic
4	slices bread (100g | 3 1/2oz)
10	peppercorns
1/2tsp	saffron
1/4tsp	cumin
	salt
1 1/2litres | 2 1/2pt	chicken broth
1tsp	vinegar
	chopped parsley

Heat the oil in a soup pot and in it toast the almonds, garlic and bread. Remove them and place in a blender or processor with the pepper, saffron, cumin and salt, reserving a few cubes of bread for garnish. Add the vinegar and a little of the broth and purée until smooth. Heat the broth in the same pot and stir in the almond mixture. Bring to the boil and simmer for 15 minutes. Garnish with chopped parsley and reserved bread cubes. Serves 4.

Variation: An almond soup typically served on *Noche Buena,* Christmas Eve, is made with sweetened almond paste, lemon peel and cinnamon. The Basques serve a similar soup made of ground walnuts.

SOPA DE PICADILLO
Noodle Soup With Ham

This is usually made with left-over broth from the *cocido* (see recipe in following chapter), a chicken and meat soup flavoured with cured ham bone. You could use tinned consommé or stock cubes instead. Cook thin soup noodles in it. Fry chopped ham in a little oil and add to the soup before serving with chopped, hard-cooked eggs and a spoonful of sherry. Serve hot, garnished with sprigs of fresh mint. Fried bread cubes or cooked rice can be substituted for the noodles.

Variation: A Catalan soup, *de galets,* substitutes large shell pasta for the noodles and replaces the ham with tiny meatballs made of minced pork and breadcrumbs seasoned with a pinch of cinnamon and nutmeg.

POTAJE DE LENTEJAS
Lentil Soup

1/2kg | 1lb	lentils
3litres | 5 1/4pt	water
6tbsp	oil
1	tomato, peeled
1	green pepper
1	onion, quartered
1	bay-leaf
1	whole head of garlic
1tbsp	salt
2	cloves
2	large potatoes, chopped
1/2tsp	paprika
1/2tsp	ground cumin
1/4tsp	ground pepper
	dash of cayenne or chilli
200g | 7oz	spicy pork sausage or Catalan *butifarra*

Cover the lentils with twice their volume of water and bring them to the boil. Leave to soak for an hour, then drain and add 3 litres fresh water. Add the oil, the peeled and chopped tomato, the green pepper cut in pieces, the quartered onion and bay-leaf. Roast the head of garlic by holding it with tongs or a fork over an open flame or put under the grill until it is charred. Peel the garlic cloves and add to the lentils with the salt. Bring to the boil and simmer for an hour. Then add the potatoes, paprika, cumin, pepper and cayenne. Add the sausages and cook the lentils until everything is tender, another 40 minutes. The greenish-brown lentils will cook almost to a purée; the tiny, nearly-black ones keep their shape. Serves 6.

SOPA DE PESCADOS Y MARISCOS
Seafood Soup

2kg | 4 1/2lb	whole fish, 2 or more varieties
1kg | 2lb	shellfish — lobster, prawns, crayfish, crab
1kg | 2lb	clams, mussels, scallops or other bivalves
1	squid (200g | 7oz), cleaned
3litres | 5 1/4pt	water
100ml | 3 1/2fl oz	white wine
	salt and pepper
1	small onion
1	carrot
1	stalk celery
	bay-leaf, thyme, parsley
4tbsp	oil
1	clove garlic, minced
6tbsp	brandy
2	slices bread
1/2tsp	saffron
10	peppercorns
	cayenne
1/4litre | 1/2pt	tomato sauce
	chopped parsley
	triangles of fried bread

Have the fish vendor fillet the fish, saving all the heads, bones and trimmings. Cut the fillets into chunks, removing any remaining bones, and set aside. Shell the prawns or slice the halved lobster, remove the shells and hack the shells and head into pieces. Scrub the clams, mussels, etc., and steam them open over a high heat in a covered pan. Remove and discard the shells, reserving the flesh. Strain the liquid and reserve it. Put all the fish trimmings and crustacean shells into a large pot with the water, white wine, salt and pepper, half the onion, carrot, celery and herbs. Bring to the boil, skim the froth and simmer, partially covered, for an hour. Meanwhile, in another pot or deep casserole, heat the oil and in it sauté the remaining onion, finely minced, and the garlic. Add the pieces of fish and sauté them, then add the peeled prawns or pieces of lobster and the clams or mussels. Pour over the brandy and set it alight, stirring until flames subside. Toast the bread or fry it in a little oil. Put it in a blender with the saffron, peppercorns, cayenne and a little of the fish stock and whirl until smooth. Add to the fish with the tomato sauce. Strain the prepared stock and add about 10 cups of it to the fish. Simmer the soup for 10 minutes. Serve, sprinkled with chopped parsley and garnished with fried bread triangles. Serves 6-8.

Tip: Use both firm-fleshed fish such as angler *(rape)*, sea bass *(lubina)*, rockfish *(gallineta, cabracho, rubio)*, and flaky ones such as hake *(merluza)* and its relations, cod, whiting, haddock; sole *(lenguado)*, or bream *(besugo)*.

SUQUET DEL PESCADOR
Catalan Fishermen's Soup

1 1/2-2kg | 3 1/2-4 1/2lb	whole fish or 3/4kg | 1 3/4lb fillets
4tbsp	olive oil
3	cloves garlic, crushed
1	tomato, peeled and chopped
2	onions, thinly sliced
4	potatoes, peeled
2litres | 3 1/2pt	water or fumet
100ml | 3 1/2fl oz	white wine
	salt
3tbsp	chopped parsley
	alioli sauce (garlic mayonnaise, see recipe page 21)

Typically the fish would be cut into crosswise slices, bones and all, but you can use bone-free fillets if preferred. Save head and trimmings to make fish stock. Place the oil, crushed garlic, chopped tomato, sliced onions and sliced potatoes in a deep earthenware casserole or soup pot. Cover with the water or fumet and add the wine. Bring to the boil and cook for 5 minutes. Add the pieces of fish and sprinkle with salt. Cook on a very hot fire until fish flakes and potatoes are tender, about 10 minutes more. Sprinkle with the chopped parsley and serve the soup from the same casserole. Accompany with *alioli* sauce. Serves 6.

SOPA AL CUARTO DE HORA
Fifteen-Minute Fish Soup

4tbsp	olive oil
1	small onion, minced
1	tomato, peeled and chopped
1 1/2litres | 2 1/2pt	water or fish stock
1/2tsp	crushed saffron
125g | 4oz	serrano ham
6tbsp	dry sherry
100g | 3 1/2oz	rice
75g | 2 1/2oz	shelled peas
1	dozen steamed clams
150g | 5oz	shelled prawns
150g | 5oz	fish fillets
	salt and pepper
2	hard-cooked eggs, chopped
	chopped parsley

Heat the oil in a soup pot and in it sauté the chopped onion.
Add the peeled and chopped tomato, the fish stock, crushed
saffron, diced ham, sherry, rice and peas and bring to the boil.
Cook on a high heat for 10 minutes, then lower heat and add
the clams, prawns, and pieces of fish. Season with salt and
pepper and cook 5 minutes more. Serve with chopped, hard-
cooked eggs and chopped parsley. Serves 4.

SOPA MALAGUEÑA
Sherried Fish Soup, Málaga Style

2litres | 3 1/2pt	water or fish stock
1/2kg | 1lb	fish fillets
1/4kg | 9oz	shelled prawns
50g | 2oz	shelled peas
30g | 1oz	serrano ham, diced
1	red pimento
1/4litre | 1/2pint	mayonnaise
2tbsp	lemon juice
5tbsp	dry sherry
	salt and pepper
	lemon for garnish

Heat the water or stock in a soup pot, reduce to a simmer and add the pieces of fish. Cook just until flaky, about 5 minutes. Remove from heat and remove the fish from the broth. Cut into chunks and set aside. Add the peas, ham and diced red pimento to the soup. Cook until peas are tender, 5 minutes. Meanwhile, beat the mayonnaise in a bowl with the lemon juice and sherry until smooth and creamy. Add the prawns to the soup and keep at a low simmer. Ladle a cupful of hot soup into the mayonnaise, whisking constantly, then whisk this mixture into the soup. Heat very briefly, but do not boil. Add the reserved pieces of fish. Serve hot with lemon slices. Serves 6.

SOPA DE RAPE
Anglerfish Soup

1	whole anglerfish, 1 1/2kg | 3 1/2lb (or 1/2kg | 1lb fillets)
3litres | 5 1/4pt	water
	bay, parsley, oregano, thyme, celery
	salt and pepper
1	onion
4tbsp	olive oil
20	almonds, blanched and skinned
10	hazelnuts, skinned
3	cloves garlic
3	slices bread (75g | 2 1/2oz)
1	sprig parsley
2	tomatoes, peeled and chopped
1/2tsp	saffron
	grating of nutmeg
1/8tsp	cinnamon

Have the anglerfish (or monkfish) cleaned and the head separated from the tail. Put the water to boil in a pot with the herbs, half an onion, salt and pepper. Add the head and any fish trimmings and cook for 30 minutes on a hot fire. Reduce to a simmer and add the rest of the fish. Poach it for 10 minutes and remove from heat. Strain the stock and reserve. Remove bones from the cooked fish and break it into small pieces. Remove any bits of flesh from the remainder and discard head and bones.

Heat the oil in a deep earthenware casserole or soup pot. Fry the almonds, hazelnuts, garlic and bread until lightly toasted. With a skimmer, remove them to a blender or processor. In the same oil, fry the chopped, remaining onion just until softened. Add the tomatoes and fry another 15 minutes until reduced. Transfer this sauce to the blender with the nuts. Add the saffron, nutmeg, cinnamon, salt and pepper and process until smooth, adding a little of the reserved stock. Return this paste to the soup pot and stir in the stock. Bring to the boil and simmer 10 minutes, then add the pieces of cooked fish and simmer another minute or two to reheat. Serves 6-8.

Gazpachos are the cold salad-soups of Andalusia. They come red with tomatoes, green with avocados, and white with almonds.

GAZPACHO ANDALUZ
Andalusian Summertime Soup

1	thick slice bread (75g | 2 1/2oz)
1kg | 2lb	ripe tomatoes (4 large)
3	cloves garlic
2tsp	salt
1/4tsp	ground cumin
70ml |2 1/2fl oz	olive oil
5tbsp	wine vinegar
1/2litre | 1pint	water, approx.
1	green pepper
1	cucumber
1	onion
1	small tomato
2	slices bread, cubed, toasted
1	hard-cooked egg

Remove crusts from bread and soak in water to cover for 15 minutes. Squeeze out excess water and put the bread in the blender with the tomatoes, garlic, salt and cumin. Process until puréed (process in two or more batches if necessary). With the motor running, add the oil in a slow stream, then add the vinegar. The mixture will thicken and change colour as the oil emulsifies. Add a little of the water and sieve the mixture (otherwise, peel and seed tomatoes before processing). Transfer to a tureen and stir in the water. Chill until serving time. Chop the green pepper, cucumber, onion and tomato. Either add them to the chilled gazpacho or serve along with the breadcrumbs and chopped egg in small bowls to accompany it. Serves 6.

Tip: Use left-over gazpacho as a salad dressing or add dissolved gelatine and chill it in a decorative mould.

Variation: SALMOREJO CORDOBES. Make gazpacho as above without adding water. Put the thick sauce in individual bowls and top with chopped *serrano* ham and hard-cooked eggs. Serve with chunks of bread, raw cucumber and pepper strips.

AJO BLANCO CON UVAS
White Garlic Soup With Grapes

3	thick slices bread (200g | 7oz)
100g	3 1/2oz	almonds, blanched and skinned
4	cloves garlic
150ml	1/4pt	extra virgin olive oil
5tbsp	vinegar
2tsp	salt
1 1/2litres/2 1/2pt	water
200g	7oz	seeded grapes

Remove crusts from bread and soak in water until softened. Squeeze it out and put in blender or processor with the almonds and peeled garlic. (To skin almonds, put them in boiling water for 1 minute, drain and slip skins off.) Blend to a smooth sauce, adding a little water if necessary. With the motor running, add the oil in a slow stream. Then add the vinegar and salt. Beat in some of the water, then pour the contents of the blender into a tureen and add the remaining water. Taste for seasoning, adding more salt or vinegar if necessary. The soup should be quite tangy. Chill the soup. It will separate on standing, so stir it thoroughly before serving garnished with the seeded grapes, a marvellous contrast to the garlic and almonds.

Variation: Add the flesh of 2 peeled avocados to the blender with the bread and almonds, plus a drop of almond extract. Garnish with melon balls and chopped ham instead of grapes.

SALADS

Salads make an important part of Spanish meals. Many special ones are served as tapas (see previous chapter). Mixed green salads often precede a meal in place of a starter. Typically, a big platter of lettuce with tomatoes, onions and other ingredients is placed in the centre of the table and dressed at table with olive oil, vinegar, salt and pepper. Everyone eats from the same dish. When finished, chunks of bread are used to mop up the delicious "broth" in the bottom of the dish. Try it!

ENSALADA MIXTA A LA ESPAÑOLA
Spanish Mixed Salad

Wash and drain 2 heads of Boston or cabbage lettuce. Tear or shred leaves and cover a large platter with them. Top with tomatoes cut in wedges, onions thinly sliced from stem to root, peeled and sliced cucumber. Drain the contents of a can of tuna (190g | 6 1/2oz) and spoon chunks of it over the lettuce. Rinse and drain a can of white asparagus and lay one spear per person across the salad. Cut two hard-cooked eggs into quarters and garnish the salad. Finish with a dozen or so whole green olives (preferably the split and home-cured ones). Serve with cruets of olive oil, wine vinegar, salt and pepper, and fresh bread. Serves 6-8.

Variation: XATO, Catalan salad. Use chicory (curly endive) instead of lettuce. Add tinned artichokes or palm hearts, sliced tomatoes, onions. Make *romesco* sauce (see previous chapter), omitting the bread and thinning slightly with water or vinegar. Dress the salad and let it sit for 20 minutes. Serve with sliced ham or sausage.

VINAGRETA
Vinaigrette

If you prefer to pre-mix your salad dressing: combine 1 clove of crushed garlic in a bowl with 1/4 teaspoon salt and freshly ground pepper. Stir in 4 tablespoons wine vinegar, then whisk in slowly 150ml | 5fl oz extra virgin olive oil. The sauce will thicken and emulsify, but will separate if left to sit. Add chopped parsley or other fresh herb to taste. Mashed egg yolk can be added with the crushed garlic for a thicker sauce.

STARTERS

Seafood in small portions, egg and vegetable dishes make up the Spanish first course menu. Many of these excellent dishes could easily serve as a main entrée for brunch, luncheon or light supper.

Entremeses are the Spanish rendition of *hors-d'oeuvres variés* or *antipasta* — a selection of charcuterie, salads, shellfish, and perhaps one or two hot titbits such as croquettes. Entremeses are often especially good at Spain's national paradors, many of which are situated in historic buildings.

JAMON CON MELON O HIGOS
Ham With Melon or Figs

Serve chilled Spanish melon or chilled, peeled and quartered ripe figs topped with thin slices of *serrano* ham. For parties, spear cubes of melon and ham on toothpicks.

AGUACATE CON SALPICON DE MARISCOS
Avocado and Shellfish Cocktail

2	ripe avocados
2	large tomatoes
1/2	medium onion
1	green bell pepper
1	clove garlic, crushed
	dash of Tabasco
1tsp	salt
2	hard-cooked eggs
5tbsp	wine vinegar
6tbsp	olive oil
2tbsp	chopped parsley
400g | 14oz	cooked prawns, lobster, mussels, scallops, fish, etc.

Peel and pit the avocados. Slice them lengthwise and arrange the slices in a fan on 4-6 salad plates. Sprinkle with lemon juice. Chop the tomatoes, onions, green and red peppers and mix them in a bowl. Chop the egg whites and add to the salad. Mix the garlic, Tabasco, salt, egg yolks and wine vinegar in a bowl. Beat in the oil until the dressing is emulsified. Add the chopped parsley and stir into the chopped tomato mixture. Add the cooked shellfish. Spoon the salad over the sliced avocados. Serves 6-8.

Tip: Use left-over cooked fish and shellfish for this piquant salad.

BONITO A LA BILBAINA
Bonito, Bilbao Style

1	bonito, about 1 1/4kg | 2 3/4lb
1/2litre | 1pt	water
1tsp	salt
100ml | 3 1/2fl oz	white wine
1tbsp	vinegar
1	bay-leaf
1	clove garlic, slivered
	a few peppercorns
	a few sprigs of parsley
1	onion
2	hard-cooked eggs
1tbsp	chopped parsley
1tbsp	capers
1tbsp	chopped pickles
	lettuce, tomato, cucumber, lemon

Bonito is a small version of tuna. Fresh tuna steaks can be used instead. Clean the bonito and cut it into thick slices. Place them in a pan with the water, salt, wine, vinegar, bay, garlic, pepper, parsley and one slice of onion. Bring to the boil, lower the heat and simmer 10 minutes. Remove from the heat and let the fish cool in the liquid. Chop the eggs and mix with chopped half onion, chopped parsley, capers and pickles. Arrange lettuce on a serving platter or individual plates. Remove fish from liquid, draining well. Carefully remove and discard skin and bones, keeping the slices intact. Place them on the lettuce and spoon over the chopped mixture. Garnish the dish with sliced tomato, cucumber and lemon. Accompany with mayonnaise thinned with lemon juice. Serves 6 as an hors-d'oeuvre.

ESCABECHE DE PESCADO
Cold Pickled Fish

This is usually made with mackerel *(caballa)*, though other blue fish such as bonito, tuna, sardine, yellowtail or amberjack could also be used.

1kg | 2lb	fresh mackerel (about 600g | 1 1/4lb fillets)
	flour
	olive oil for frying
5	cloves garlic
50ml | 2fl oz	olive oil
2	bay-leaves
	pinch thyme
1tsp	oregano
1	clove
5	peppercorns
1	chilli pepper (optional)
1tsp	paprika
125ml | 1/4pt	vinegar
125ml | 1/4pt	water
1/4litre | 1/2pt	white wine
1tsp	salt

Have the fish cleaned and filleted. Cut the fillets crosswise into slices. Dust them with flour and fry in just enough oil to cover the bottom of the pan, adding more as necessary. Brown the pieces on both sides, remove and let cool. Place the fish in a glass or earthenware jar or bowl. Add the remaining oil to the pan and in it heat the peeled cloves of garlic, bay-leaf, thyme, oregano, cloves, peppercorns and chilli. Stir in the paprika, vinegar, water, wine and salt. Bring to the boil and lower heat to simmer for 2 minutes. Remove from heat and cool completely. Pour this pickling marinade over the fish. Cover and marinate, refrigerated, for at least 24 hours. Serve at room temperature garnished with lettuce, tomatoes, sliced onions, peppers and black olives. Makes 8-10 hors-d'oeuvre servings.

TXANGURRO
Crab Gratin, Basque Style

4	spider crabs or 100g | 3 1/2oz per person of tinned crab
4tbsp	olive oil
1	onion, minced
100ml | 3 1/2fl oz	brandy
100ml | 31/2fl oz	white wine
5tbsp	tomato sauce
1tbsp	chopped parsley
	salt and pepper
	dash cayenne
4tbsp	breadcrumbs
	butter

The crabs should be alive when purchased and weigh about 1/2kg | 1lb each. Bring a large pot of water to the boil; put the crabs in and boil them for 15 minutes. Plunge into cold water and drain. When cool, twist off legs and claws. Pry the body away from the shell. Discard the mouth, stomach bag and spongy gills. Save the soft brown meat in the shell, and the liquid. Discard hard protuberances and extract remaining meat. Scoop white meat from leg sockets. Crack the claws and legs and remove flesh from them. Clean the shells and oil them for use as baking dishes. In a frying pan sauté the onion in the oil until soft. Add the dark meat from the crab. Pour over the brandy, set it alight and stir gently until flames subside. Add the wine, tomato sauce, parsley, salt and pepper and cayenne and simmer about 15 minutes, adding a little water or stock if sauce seems too thick. Add the remaining crabmeat to the sauce and spoon it into 2 or 4 of the prepared shells. Top with breadcrumbs and dot with butter. Put under the grill or in the top of a very hot oven until lightly browned, about 5 minutes.

Tip: One crab does not provide a lot of meat. Extend the casserole by adding 200g | 7oz boneless, cooked and flaked fish to the crab. *Rape,* anglerfish, is a good choice.

Variation: VIEIRAS A LA GALLEGA, scallops, Galician style. Use the meat from 2kg | 4 1/2lb sea scallops *(coquilles St. Jacques),* unshelled, or 1/2kg | 1lb shelled, in place of the crab, adding it to the sauce after simmering. Pile in scallop shells and gratiné.

ANGULAS AL PIL PIL
Sizzling Baby Eels

The consumption of tiny elvers, *angulas,* is almost an obsession in the Basque country. They are essential for holiday meals. In Spain you can buy them cooked and frozen. The elvers are only a few centimetres long, thin, and nearly transparent.

For 1 serving: place 3 tablespoons oil in a small earthenware casserole with 1 clove garlic, coarsely chopped, and a small piece of chilli pepper. Heat until the oil is very hot. Add 150g l 5oz of elvers and toss them in the oil with a wooden spoon only until they are thoroughly heated and the oil is bubbling, 2 minutes. Add 1 teaspoon water and serve immediately while the oil is still sizzling.

SARDINAS A LA ESPAÑOLA
Sardines, Spanish Style

1kg | 2lb	fresh sardines
1	medium onion
1	green pepper
2	large tomatoes
2	cloves garlic
2tbsp	chopped parsley
1	chilli pepper (optional)
1/4tsp	saffron
1/4tsp	cumin
1/4tsp	paprika
	salt and pepper
2tbsp	white wine
3tbsp	oil
	toast or fried bread

Clean the sardines, remove scales, heads and spines. Wash and pat dry. Chop together (use processor, if available) the onion, pepper, tomatoes, garlic, parsley and chilli. Add the crushed saffron, ground cumin, paprika and salt and pepper. In an oven dish spread half the chopped vegetables and lay the filleted sardines on top. Cover with another layer of the chopped vegetables. Drizzle with the oil. Cover and bake in a hot oven until the sardines are cooked, about 30 minutes.

Serve hot or cold as an hors-d'oeuvre with toast points or fried bread. Garnish with a few olives and lemon slices.

Variation: with tinned Spanish sardines. Make a sauce by frying the tomatoes and other vegetables in a little oil with the seasoning until thickened, about 15 minutes. Drain tinned sardines of oil and add them to the sauce. Simmer for 3 minutes and remove from heat. Leave them in the tomato sauce several hours before serving with a squeeze of lemon.

PIMIENTOS DE PIQUILLO RELLENOS
CON PESCADO
Piquant Peppers Stuffed With Fish

These peppers are slightly smaller than bell peppers, with a pointy bottom and a slight "bite" or piquancy. If fresh, they are roasted and peeled; more usually, they are purchased tinned.

8	pimentos (460g | 1lb)
300g | 10oz	cooked fish or shellfish
3tbsp	butter or oil
1/2	onion, minced
1	clove garlic, minced
3tbsp	flour
1/2litre/1pt	milk
	grating of fresh nutmeg
	salt and pepper
	dash of cayenne
8tbsp	white wine
1tsp	paprika

Heat the butter or oil in a saucepan and sauté the minced onion and garlic until softened, about 2 minutes. Stir in the flour and cook, stirring, a further 2 minutes. Whisk in the milk and season with nutmeg, salt, pepper and cayenne. Cook, stirring constantly, until sauce is thickened, about 8 minutes. Set aside about 5 tablespoons of the sauce. Add half the sauce to the cooked fish or shellfish, flaked or chopped. Drain and rinse the pimentos. Very carefully fill them with the fish mixture and place in an oiled oven dish. Stir the reserved sauce with the white wine and paprika and cook 5 minutes. Pour over the stuffed peppers. Cover and bake in a medium oven for 15 minutes or until heated through.

Variation: Use minced ham or cooked pork instead of fish. Roll the stuffed peppers in flour, dip in beaten egg, and dredge in breadcrumbs. Fry them in a little oil until browned on all sides.

EGG DISHES

Serve these egg dishes as a starter or light entrée, not just for breakfast. The classic Spanish tortilla (see preceding chapter) is a versatile omelette with potatoes or other vegetables, served round and flat rather than folded like a French omelette. A *revuelto* is egg soft-scrambled with other ingredients.

REVUELTO DE SETAS
Eggs Scrambled With Wild Mushrooms

150g | 50z	wild mushrooms
2tbsp	oil
1	clove garlic, minced
4	eggs
1tbsp	chopped parsley
1tbsp	water
	salt and pepper

Clean the mushrooms and dry them. Cut them into small pieces. Sauté them in a frying pan in the oil. Some types of wild mushrooms give off a lot of water. Continue cooking until most of the water has evaporated. Add the minced garlic and fry briefly. Beat the eggs together with the parsley, water, salt and pepper and pour them into the pan with the mushrooms, adding a little more oil as needed. Continue stirring the egg mixture until it is just set; still soft and creamy. Serve immediately with strips of fried bread. Serves 2.

REVUELTO DE AJETES
Garlic-Scrambled Eggs

Ajetes are tender young shoots of garlic, which look like scallions or green onions. If you can't get the real thing, substitute scallions, adding a clove of garlic, crushed, to the eggs.

150g | 5oz	garlic shoots
3tbsp	olive oil
4	eggs
	pinch of thyme
	salt and pepper
1tbsp	chopped parsley

Clean the garlic shoots and chop them. Heat the oil in a frying pan and sauté the garlic very gently, without letting it brown, about 10 minutes. In a bowl beat the eggs with the thyme, salt and pepper and chopped parsley. Pour them into the pan and stir over a low heat until the eggs are set, but still soft and creamy. Serve immediately. Serves 2.

DUELOS Y QUEBRANTOS
Eggs Scrambled With Bacon and Sausage

A dish from La Mancha, this is what the legendary Don Quixote ate on Saturday nights.

50g | 2oz	salt pork, bacon or fatty ham
50g | 2oz	chorizo sausage
1tbsp	olive oil
4	eggs
2tbsp	water or milk
	salt and pepper

Cut the salt pork, bacon or ham into small dice. Remove sausage casing and cut chorizo into small pieces. Fry pork and sausage in a little oil in a frying pan. Beat the eggs with water or milk, season with salt and pepper and stir into the pan. Scramble the eggs until soft-set and serve with triangles of bread fried in olive oil. Serves 2 or 3.

PIPERRADA
Basque Eggs Scrambled With Peppers

2	red bell peppers
6tbsp	olive oil
4	cloves garlic
1	small onion, chopped

50g	2oz	chopped ham
2	tomatoes, chopped
8	eggs
	salt and pepper

Roast the peppers under the grill or on a gas flame until they are charred on all sides. Wrap them in a clean kitchen towel until they are cooled, then peel off the skin. Discard seeds and stem and cut the peppers into strips. Heat the oil in a frying pan and sauté the chopped garlic and onions. Add the chopped ham, then the peeled and chopped tomatoes with the strips of pepper and fry for 15 minutes until reduced to a sauce. Remove and set aside. Beat the eggs with the salt and pepper. Add a little more oil to the pan and pour in the eggs. Stir them, cooking very gently, until they are just barely set. Spoon the pepper mixture over them, stirring to blend. Cover and cook another minute or two. Serves 4.

ZARANGOLLO
Levant Eggs With Courgette

1kg	2lb	courgettes
2	onions
6tbsp	oil
6	eggs, beaten
	salt and pepper

Slice the courgettes thinly. Slice the onions. Place both in a colander, salt lightly, and let drain for 20 minutes. Heat the oil in a frying pan and add the vegetables. Cook slowly until the courgettes are tender, about 10 minutes. Use a spatula to turn them gently as they cook. Beat the eggs with salt and pepper and pour into the pan. Let cook just until the eggs are set. Turn out on to a serving dish and garnish with chopped green onions or chopped fresh herbs. Serves 4.

Variation: Use sliced aubergine instead of courgettes. After adding eggs, cook on both sides as for a Spanish omelette.

HUEVOS A LA FLAMENCA
Flamenco Eggs

100g | 3 1/2oz	chorizo, sliced
4tbsp	olive oil
1	small onion, chopped
1	clove garlic, minced
3	tomatoes, chopped
8	eggs
75g | 2 1/2oz	cooked peas
8	cooked asparagus tips
2	cooked artichokes
1	tinned red pimento
	salt and pepper
	chopped parsley
50g | 2oz	ham

Fry the sliced chorizo in a little of the oil until warmed through. Remove it and reserve. Add remaining oil to the pan and in it brown the chopped onion and garlic. Add the chopped tomatoes, season with salt and pepper, and cook on a medium heat until reduced to a sauce, about 12 minutes. Oil 4 ramekins or individual baking dishes. Divide the tomato sauce between them. Make 2 indentations in the sauce and break an egg into each. Cut the ham in strips and arrange around the eggs. Sprinkle a few cooked peas over each ramekin; arrange 2 asparagus tips and half an artichoke around the eggs and garnish with the sliced chorizo. Lay strips of red pimento over all. Bake the eggs in a preheated medium-hot oven until the whites are set, about 10 minutes. Serve immediately with triangles of bread fried in olive oil.

VEGETABLE STARTERS

Vegetables in Spanish cookery often appear as starters. Some of them are substantial enough to make light luncheon entrées.

ALCACHOFAS SALTEADAS
Sautéd Artichokes

12	artichokes or 1 package frozen (400g | 14oz)
2tsp	lemon juice
1tsp	salt
	flour
6tbsp	olive oil
100g	3 1/2oz	diced ham
2	cloves garlic
	salt and pepper

Trim off the outer leaves of the artichokes, cut off the tops and cut the bottoms into quarters. Rub all the surfaces with a cut lemon. Cook in boiling salted water with the lemon juice until barely tender. Drain well and pat dry. Dredge the pieces of artichoke in flour. Heat the olive oil in a frying pan and add the pieces of artichoke, diced ham and chopped garlic. Fry until browned. Season with salt and pepper and serve with wedges of lemon. If using frozen artichokes, thaw them, cut into pieces, then flour and fry.

ALCACHOFAS CON ALMEJAS A LA MONTILLA
Artichokes and Clams With Montilla

12	artichokes or 1 package frozen (400g | 14oz)
6tbsp	olive oil
1	slice bread
6	cloves garlic
1/4tsp	toasted saffron
1tsp	paprika
100ml	3 1/2oz	dry Montilla wine (or sherry)
400g	14oz	clams
	sprigs of mint
150ml	1/4pt	water

Trim off outer leaves and cut off tops of artichokes. Cut them into quarters and rub with lemon juice to prevent their darkening. Cook the artichokes in boiling salted water with some lemon juice until nearly tender. Drain well and reserve. In a frying pan or earthenware casserole heat the oil and in it fry the bread and peeled garlic until toasted. Remove them to a mortar or processor with the toasted saffron and Montilla (or sherry) wine and process until smooth. Add the drained artichokes to the oil with the clams, scrubbed clean, and fry them for 3 minutes. Add the sauce from the processor and the water. Stir and simmer until clams are opened. Garnish with sprigs of mint. Serves 4.

Variation: If ever you should encounter cardoons, *cardos,* a vegetable which looks like celery and tastes like artichoke, use it in this recipe instead of artichokes.

HABAS CON JAMON A LA GRANADINA
Broad Beans With Ham, Granada Style

2kg | 4 1/2lb	broad beans
100ml | 3 1/2fl oz	olive oil
150g | 5oz	serrano ham, diced
5	cloves garlic, chopped
	salt and pepper
	chopped parsley, fennel or mint

Shell the beans (or use 2 packages frozen broad beans). Heat the oil in an earthenware or other flame-proof casserole. Add the beans, diced ham and chopped garlic. Fry briefly on a very high heat, then reduce the heat and let the beans stew in the oil until they are quite tender, about 20 minutes. A little water can be added as needed. Season with salt and pepper to taste and sprinkle with one of the chopped herbs. Serves 6.

CAZUELA DE VERDURAS
Vegetable Casserole

6	artichokes
2kg | 4 1/2lb	broad beans
5tbsp	olive oil
1	slice bread
6	cloves garlic
12	small new potatoes
1	small onion, chopped
2	tomatoes, chopped
	bay-leaf, parsley and mint
1/4tsp	saffron
1/2tsp	cumin
6	peppercorns
	salt
6	eggs

Trim off outer leaves from artichokes and cut off tops. Cut them in half, rub with cut lemon and drop into boiling, salted, acidulated water. Cook for 10 minutes and drain. Shell the beans and blanch them for 5 minutes. Drain and set aside. Heat the oil in an earthenware or flame-proof casserole and in it fry the bread and garlic until toasted. Remove them and set aside. Add the potatoes and chopped onion to the oil and fry until slightly browned. Add the beans and artichokes, the tomatoes and the herbs. Add enough water to barely cover. Cover the casserole and simmer. In a mortar or blender crush the saffron, cumin and peppercorns with the fried bread and garlic. Dilute with a little of the liquid from the vegetables and add to the casserole. Season to taste with salt and cook until beans are tender, 30 minutes. Break eggs on top of the vegetables and bake until the whites are just set, about 8 minutes in a hot oven. Garnish with chopped parsley or mint.

MAIN DISHES

THE DISH BEST LOVED by Spaniards is the *cocido,* which is both first and main courses, all cooked in one pot. The affluent eat *cocido* for festive meals, when it is a cornucopia of meats, sausages, fowl, vegetables and pasta. Frugal housewives serve it as daily fare, for ingredients can be stretched to feed large families. The *cocido* is Spanish "soul food," sustaining of both body and spirit.

COCIDO
Two-Course Dinner-in-a-Pot

In Madrid and much of Castile, this is the classic *cocido.* In Catalonia, they call it *escudella i carn d'olla* and add a huge meat dumpling. In Andalusia it's *puchero* and is probably flavoured with a *sofrito* of fried tomato, onion and garlic. The Basque cocido calls for red beans instead of the *garbanzos* or chick-peas used elsewhere and the Galician version, *pote gallego,* uses the favoured turnip greens instead of cabbage. In the Canary Islands sweetcorn and sweet potatoes lend an exotic touch.

3litres | 5 1/4pt	water
400g | 14oz	stewing beef
1	beef shin bone
100g | 3 1/2oz	salt pork
1	meaty ham bone
1/4kg | 1/2lb	garbanzos, soaked overnight
2	carrots
1	turnip
2	leeks
1	stalk celery
1	onion
2	cloves
2kg | 4 1/2lb	stewing hen
2tsp	salt
100g | 3 1/2oz	minced beef or pork
2	slices bread, soaked
1	clove garlic, minced
1	beaten egg
	salt and pepper
6	medium potatoes
1	small cabbage
150g | 5oz	morcilla (black pudding)
150g | 5oz	chorizo sausage
150g | 5oz	fine noodles, rice or bread
	parsley and mint
	tomato sauce

Put the water in a large soup pot and add the stewing beef, shin bone, salt pork and ham bone. (Some cocidos require cured meats such as ham, ribs, trotters. These should be soaked overnight in water to desalt them.) Bring to the boil and skim. Drain the garbanzos which have been soaked overnight and add to the pot with the stewing hen, peeled carrots and turnip, cleaned leeks, celery and the onion stuck with cloves. Keep skimming off the froth as the liquid boils. Then reduce to a simmer. Cover and cook for an hour. Add the salt and continue cooking.

Meanwhile, mix the minced beef or pork with the bread, soaked in water and squeezed out. Season with garlic, 1 tablespoon chopped parsley, salt and pepper and add the beaten egg. Form into small balls — the *relleno* — and brown them in a little oil in a frying pan. Add them to the cocido during the last 20 minutes of cooking.

In a separate pot, using some of the broth from the cocido or with additional water, cook the potatoes, cut in pieces; the cabbage, cut in wedges or coarsely chopped; the black pudding and chorizo sausage, until potatoes are very tender, about 30 minutes.

Strain some of the broth from the first pot into another pan. Bring it to the boil and cook in it the fine noodles or rice. If using bread instead, remove crusts, cut into strips and place in soup plates. Ladle the broth into the plates and garnish with chopped parsley or mint and serve as the meal's first course. Some of the liquid from the cabbage pot can be added, if desired. In Andalusia, the soup would include the garbanzos. For the main course, serve a platter of the drained garbanzos, carrots, turnip, leeks, celery, onion, potatoes and cabbage. Cut the beef, chicken, sausages, salt pork and ham into pieces and serve them on a second platter with the meat dumplings. Accompany with tomato sauce. Serves 6-8.

In Spain soups, stews and potages often precede a main dish of fish or meat. However, many of them are hearty enough to serve as a meal's main course.

LACON CON GRELOS
Cured Pork With Greens

A Galician dish. *Lacón* is salt-cured pork hand or shoulder and *grelos* are flowering turnip tops. Ham could be substituted for the shoulder; turnip greens, collards, or even cabbage for the grelos. This dish often includes other salt-cured meats, such as trotters, hocks, ears, cheeks. Soak salt meats overnight before cooking.

1kg | 2lb	cured pork shoulder or ham, soaked to desalt
1 1/2kg | 3 1/4lb	greens
400g | 14oz	chorizo sausage
12	small potatoes
	salt and pepper

Put the soaked pork shoulder to cook in plenty of water to cover. Bring to the boil, skim the froth, then simmer until the meat is tender, about 1 1/2 hours. Wash the greens, chop them into pieces and add to the pot. Add the chorizo and cook 10 minutes, then add the potatoes, peeled and left whole. Taste and add salt if necessary. Cook until potatoes and greens are tender, about 30 minutes. With a skimmer, remove greens to a serving platter. Cut the meat into pieces and put on top of the greens. Arrange chorizo and potatoes around the side of the dish. Serves 6.

FABADA
Ham and Beans

An Asturian dish, usually made with salt-cured *lacón,* or pork shoulder, but ham or back bacon can be substituted. The black pudding and chorizo should be smoked if possible. The *fabes* are big, white beans. You could use dry butter beans or lima beans instead.

1/2kg | 1lb	dry butter beans, soaked overnight
400g | 14oz	black pudding
400g | 14oz	chorizo
400g | 14oz	cured ham or shoulder
150g | 5oz	salt pork or streaky bacon
1/4tsp	saffron
1	bay-leaf

The previous day, put the beans to soak in water to cover. Put the salt-cured ham or shoulder to soak in hot water. Blanch the salt pork in boiling water. The following day, wash sausages to eliminate excess smokiness. Drain beans and put them in a deep earthenware casserole or large cooking pot and add water to cover the beans by a depth of two fingers. Bring to the boil and skim off the froth. Toast the saffron lightly and crush it in a mortar or teacup. Dissolve in a little water and add to the beans. Add the soaked ham and salt pork to the casserole, pushing them to the bottom of the beans. Return to the boil and skim. Then add the sausages and skim again. Add bay-leaf, then cover and cook very slowly, 2 to 3 hours, or until beans are very tender. Add cold water occasionally to just barely keep the beans covered. Do not stir. Let sit 20 minutes off the heat before serving. Serves 4.

HABAS A LA CATALANA
Catalan Broad Beans

Butifarra is Catalan sausage, white and black. If not available, use a light sausage such as bratwurst for the white, black pudding for the black.

3kg | 6 1/2lb	fresh broad beans
2tbsp	lard
150g | 5oz	streaky bacon
6	scallions
6	cloves garlic
200g | 7oz	white butifarra
200g | 7oz	black butifarra
	salt and pepper
	bouquet garni of thyme, bay, mint, cinnamon
50ml | 2fl oz	medium sherry
2tbsp	anise brandy
	chopped parsley or mint

Shell the beans. Heat the lard in a soup pot or deep earthenware casserole. Cut the piece of bacon into several pieces and brown it in the fat. Chop the scallions and add with the chopped garlic and sauté 2 minutes. Add the shelled beans, then the two kinds of sausage. Season with salt and pepper and the herb bouquet. Add the sherry, anise brandy and enough water or stock to just cover the beans. Cook them, tightly covered, until very tender, about 40 minutes. Discard the bouquet garni. Cut the sausages into pieces and arrange on top of the beans. Sprinkle with chopped parsley or mint. Serves 6.

Rice dishes are glorious in Spain and paella is queen of them all. Paella — named after the broad, shallow pan in which it is cooked — is a native of the marshy regions of eastern Spain, the Levant, near Valencia, where rice, brought to Spain by the Moors, was first grown. It probably started off as a simple country dish, containing eels, crayfish, snails, or prawns, which are still abundant in this region, plus vegetables from the fertile fields — broad beans, peas, artichokes and, later, after Columbus's great discovery, the New World treasures:

tomatoes, peppers, green beans. Saffron, a precious spice and another Moorish legacy, coloured and flavoured the rice.

Today, of course, paella in posh restaurants abroad is a fantasy dish featuring lobster, far removed from its simple beginnings. In Spain it can vary enormously, from hideous renditions served up to tourists — foreign and Spanish alike — coloured with artificial yellow colouring and with rice kernels like buckshot, to wondrous productions, replete with rabbit, prawns and clams, cooked over a wood fire on a country outing. For these fiesta paellas, men take over the cooking, with lots of good-natured arguing about ingredients and technique.

A really good paella doesn't have to contain large proportions of chicken and seafood. In fact, it's sometimes served as a first course, much as the Italians serve pasta, before the fish or meat course. Either way it's still, basically, a rice dish. Colour it yellow, add slashes of red pepper, a few pink prawns, black mussels, a scattering of green peas — it's got to look as great as it tastes.

A Spanish paella pan of rolled steel will rust. After use, scour it well, dry, and either rub with oil or dust with flour — which absorbs moisture. Store wrapped in plastic. A pan measuring 40cm/16in will serve about 8 people generously. The hard part is fitting a pan this big on an ordinary hob (try placing over two burners). If you don't have a paella pan, use your largest frying pan or a Chinese wok.

Spanish rice is a round, medium-short grain. Don't use long-grain pilaff rice for paella. If you can't get Spanish rice, substitute Italian risotto rice, *arborio* (classic Italian risotto is a spin-off of paella), or Chinese short-grain rice. Rice for paella is never washed first; the grain's starchy coating helps keep it separate.

PAELLA

1 dozen	clams or mussels
1/2kg | 1lb	prawns
1	small chicken, cut up
200g | 7oz	boneless pork
75ml | 2 1/2fl oz	olive oil
3	cloves garlic

1	bay-leaf
1	small onion, minced
2	green peppers
1	squid (about 300g/10oz)
2	large tomatoes, peeled
1/2kg | 1lb	rice
1 1/4litres | 2 1/4pt	hot liquid
1/2tsp	saffron (1/2g)
10	peppercorns
1/2tsp	sweet paprika
2tsp	salt
1	small tin red pimento
100g | 3 1/2oz	cooked peas

1. Scrub the clams or mussels and steam them open. Black mussel shells with their creamy-orange flesh are especially attractive. Remove a half shell and discard, reserving shellfish on one shell. Strain and reserve the liquid.

2. Peel the prawns, saving several, unpeeled, for garnish. Cook the unpeeled ones in a little water and set aside. Prawn shells can be boiled in water for 15 minutes, then strained, and the liquid reserved for cooking the rice.

3. Cut the chicken into very small serving pieces. Typically in Spain it would be hacked into tiny pieces for quick cooking, which unfortunately makes for bone splinters. If desired, wings, back and neck can be cooked separately for stock. Cut the pork into small cubes.

4. In the paella pan heat half the oil and in it toast the garlic and bay-leaf. Remove and set aside.

5. In the same oil, slowly brown the chicken pieces with the pork. The chicken should be half-cooked in the browning process.

6. Now add the minced onion, and green pepper cut in strips, to the oil. Sauté a few minutes.

7. Add the pieces of cleaned squid and fry for several minutes. (See page 23-24 for how to clean squid.)

8. Add the chopped tomatoes and raise heat to high so that they "fry" in the oil. Add remaining oil at this point and heat well.

9. Combine the reserved cooking liquids — prawn, mussel and chicken — plus water. You should have approximately

double the volume of liquid to rice, i.e., 2 cups rice, 4 cups liquid. Add the liquid to the paella pan and cook on a high heat.

10. In a mortar or teacup crush the saffron, peppercorns, paprika, garlic, bay-leaf and salt. Dilute with a little liquid from the pan, or in a little white wine, and add to the paella. Stir it in well. Cook on a medium heat until chicken is partially cooked, 5 minutes. Add the peeled prawns.

11. Add the rice to the boiling liquid in the pan and stir it to distribute evenly. (Or, add rice to the pan first and then add boiling liquid.)

12. Cook for a few minutes at high heat, then turn the heat down and let the paella continue cooking. Shake the pan occasionally, but do not stir the rice, as this breaks the grains. The rice will crust slightly on the bottom, but should not scorch. Add a little more liquid into the centre as necessary.

13. Decorate the top with the reserved clams and mussels on the half shell, cooked, unpeeled prawns, strips of red pimento and cooked peas.

14. Remove the paella from the heat when all the liquid is absorbed and rice still slightly resistant. Let it sit for 5-10 minutes before serving. (You may place it in a very low oven for 10 minutes.) Serve the paella with quartered lemons as garnish.

Variation: make ARROZ A LA MARINERA, all-seafood paella, omitting the chicken and pork and using sliced conger and sliced angler fish as well as prawns, clams and squid.

ARROZ CON POLLO
Rice With Chicken

This is a fine example of *arroz caldoso,* a rice casserole in which, like risotto, some liquid remains.

1	small chicken, jointed
4tbsp	olive oil
1	small onion, chopped
1	red bell pepper, chopped
1	green bell pepper, chopped
100g | 3 1/2oz	mushrooms, sliced
200g | 7oz	green beans, parboiled
1	tin tomatoes (800g | 1 3/4lb)

250g | 9oz	rice
1/2tsp	saffron
1tsp	cumin
1/2tsp	paprika
1/2tsp	thyme
1/2tsp	peppercorns
4	cloves garlic
1 litre | 1 3/4pt	hot chicken stock
	salt
2	artichokes, quartered and cooked
1	tinned red pimento
2	dozen green olives, pitted

Use the bony pieces of chicken to make a stock, boiling them with carrot, onion, celery and herbs. Strain and reserve the liquid. Heat the oil in a stew pot or deep casserole and in it slowly brown the chicken pieces. When nearly browned, add the chopped onion, red and green peppers, sliced mushrooms and parboiled green beans (or use frozen peas). Fry until the onion is softened. Add the whole tin of tomatoes, breaking up the tomatoes with a fork. Cook another 5 minutes then stir in the rice. Meanwhile, in a mortar crush the saffron with the cumin, paprika, thyme, peppercorns and garlic. Dissolve in a little stock and stir into the rice. Add the hot liquid and salt to taste. Bring to the boil, then reduce heat to a simmer, cover the casserole and cook very slowly until rice is just tender, about 18 minutes. Remove from heat and let sit for 10 minutes. Garnish with cooked artichokes (boil them in salted water with lemon juice), strips of red pimento and olives. Serves 4.

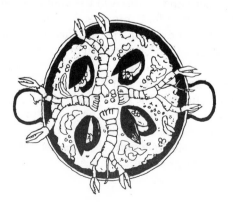

FIDEUA
Pasta Paella

Essentially, a paella made with spaghetti instead of rice, beautifully flavoured with saffron.

1 1/2litres | 2 1/2pt	fish stock
5	Dublin Bay prawns
6tbsp	olive oil
1/2kg | 1lb	angler or monk fish slices
250g | 9oz	large peeled prawns
1	squid (300g | 10oz)
1	small onion, chopped
1	green bell pepper, chopped
2	large tomatoes, peeled and chopped
100g | 3 1/2oz	shelled peas or broad beans
250g | 9oz	clams, scrubbed
1/4tsp	saffron
1/2tsp	paprika
	salt and pepper
1/2kg | 1lb	spaghetti
	sprigs of mint

Use fish heads and trimmings and prawn shells to make fish stock. Strain well. Bring to the boil and add the Dublin Bay prawns *(cigalas)*. Poach them for 5 minutes and remove. Reserve the stock. In an earthenware casserole or soup pot heat the oil. Cut the angler fish into slices, fillets or chunks and fry on both sides and remove. Add the peeled prawns, toss them briefly in the oil and remove. Add the chopped onion and chopped peppers and sauté. Add the chopped tomatoes and cook over a high heat for 2 minutes. Add the stock to the pan, bring to the boil and add the peas or broad beans and clams and the spaghetti. Crush the saffron in a mortar or teacup and mix with the paprika. Dilute in a little water or white wine and add to the casserole with salt and pepper. Lower heat to a gentle bubble and add the fried pieces of fish. When pasta is nearly cooked, 10 minutes, add the sautéd prawns. Garnish the top with the cooked Dublin Bay prawns. Remove from heat, cover the casserole and let it rest for several minutes. Garnish with sprigs of mint. Serves 6.

CAZUELA DE PATATAS
Potato-Seafood Casserole

Another in the repertoire of the *comida amarilla* — golden, saffron-hued dishes — this one with potatoes. Use either chicken and pork or fish and shellfish. *Raya*, skate, works very well, as does *rape*, angler; *cazón*, dogfish; *gallineta*, rockfish.

4tbsp	olive oil
50g | 2oz	blanched almonds (about 30)
3	cloves garlic
1	slice bread, crusts removed
1	small onion, chopped
1	green pepper, chopped
1	tomato, peeled and chopped
1/2kg | 1lb	sliced fish
250g | 9oz	scrubbed clams
10	peppercorns
2	cloves
1/4tsp	saffron
1/2tsp	paprika
1/2tsp	thyme
1tsp	salt
1 1/2kg | 3 1/2lb	potatoes
1	bay-leaf
1/2litre | 1pt	water or stock
2	artichokes, quartered and cooked

Heat the oil in an earthenware casserole or in a pot and fry the blanched almonds, garlic and bread just until toasted. Remove. Into the same oil put the chopped onion and green pepper, and sauté until softened. Add the chopped tomato and fry for 5 minutes, then add the sliced fish and cleaned clams. Fry for several minutes. Meanwhile, in a mortar or processor crush the peppercorns, cloves, saffron, paprika and thyme with the salt. Add the fried almonds, garlic and bread and process to a smooth paste, adding a little liquid if necessary. Dilute in a little stock and add to the casserole with the bay-leaf and potatoes, peeled and cut in chunks. Add the liquid. Bring to the boil and reduce heat to a simmer. Cover and cook until potatoes are tender but not mushy, adding more liquid as necessary. The casserole should be "juicy," but not soupy. Add the cooked, quartered artichokes. Remove from heat, cover, and let the casserole sit for 10 minutes before serving. Serves 6.

EMPANADA GALLEGA
Galician Pork Pie

Made with a bread dough crust, this pie is delicious hot out of the oven or packed, cold, for a picnic.

For the crust:

40g | 1 1/2oz	pressed yeast
150ml | 1/4pt	very warm water
1/2tsp	sugar
1/2kg | 1lb	flour
1tsp	salt
75g | 2 1/2oz	lard or butter
1	egg, lightly beaten

Place the yeast in a small bowl. Add the water, sugar and 3 tablespoons of the flour. Set in a warm place for about 10 minutes until bubbly. Meanwhile, place the flour in a bowl and add to it the salt and lard, mixing the fat into the flour with the fingers. Make a well in the centre and pour in the dissolved yeast and beaten egg. Use the hands to mix in the flour, then turn the dough out on to a floured board and knead until smooth and elastic, about 5 minutes. Sprinkle with additional flour to prevent dough from sticking, then pat into a ball and place in a greased bowl. Cover with a damp cloth and set in a warm place to rise until doubled in bulk, about 1 hour.

For the filling:

300g | 10oz	boneless pork loin, thinly sliced
1/2tsp	paprika
2	cloves garlic
1/2tsp	oregano
1tbsp	chopped parsley
	salt and pepper
4tbsp	oil or lard
1	green pepper, chopped
3	onions, chopped
3	tomatoes, peeled and chopped
1	tin sweet red pimentos
1	egg

Place the slices of pork loin in a dish and sprinkle with the paprika, 1 chopped clove of garlic, oregano, chopped parsley and salt and pepper. Leave to marinate for 30 minutes. Heat the oil or lard in a frying pan and fry the pork slices, browning on both sides. Remove and set aside. In the same oil sauté the chopped green pepper and onions and remaining chopped garlic until softened. Add the chopped tomatoes and season with salt and pepper. Cook until tomatoes are reduced and sauce is thick.

Divide the prepared dough in half. On a floured board roll out one half to a thickness of 2cm I 3/4in. Line a round or rectangular oven tin with the dough. Spread this with half of the prepared sauce. Arrange the slices of pork loin on top. Cut the pimentos into strips and arrange a layer of them on top. Cover with the remaining sauce. Roll out the remaining dough in the same manner. Cover the pie with it. Crimp the edges together and trim off any excess. Use any scraps of dough to roll into long cords to decorate the top of the pie, moistening them with just a little water so they stick. Make a hole in the centre for a steam vent. Put in a medium hot oven for 30 minutes. Brush the top with beaten egg and bake another 15 to 20 minutes. The crust should be golden and the pie loosened from the tin when lifted with a fork. Four main course servings or 8 snacks.

Tip: Use unbaked bread dough, kneaded with a few spoonfuls of oil; or frozen pizza dough.

Variations: Instead of pork loin, use cooked and boned chicken, tuna, sardines, eel or other fish, or minced meat.

POULTRY AND GAME

After fish, chicken *(pollo)* is favourite food in Spain. It goes into *cocido* and paella and, spit-roasted, is a fiesta-day treat. Though rural families keep free-range birds, chickens purchased in the market are battery raised. Somehow they still seem to be tastier and more tender than British or American ones. Rabbit, partridge and quail also are commercially raised. Wild birds, rabbit and hare are extensively taken in Spain and cooked in a variety of country-style dishes.

POLLO AL AJILLO
Garlic Chicken

1	chicken, jointed
	salt, pepper, paprika
1	head garlic (about 10 cloves)
75ml | 2 1/2fl oz	olive oil
2tbsp	brandy
100ml | 3 1/2fl oz	dry sherry or Montilla
1	bay-leaf

Rub the chicken pieces with salt, pepper and paprika and let them sit for 15 minutes. Peel the garlic and chop coarsely. Heat the oil in a large frying pan or earthenware casserole. Add the garlic and fry it until golden and crisp. Skim it out and reserve. Add the chicken pieces and brown them very slowly on all sides. Remove the pan from the heat, add the brandy, sherry, bay-leaf and half the fried garlic. Cover and simmer until the chicken is very tender, about 25 minutes. Serve in the casserole topped with remaining fried garlic. *Patatas fritas,* chips fried in olive oil, are usually added to the casserole. Serves 4 to 6.

POLLO EN PEPITORIA
Chicken Fricassee

1	large chicken, hen, or small turkey
4tbsp	lard or oil
20	blanched almonds
1	thick slice bread, crusts removed
6	cloves garlic
1/2tsp	saffron
10	peppercorns
	grating of fresh nutmeg
	dash of ground cloves
2	tablespoons parsley
100ml | 3 1/2fl oz	white wine or sherry
150g | 5oz	cured ham, diced
1/4litre | 1/2pt	chicken stock

	bay-leaf and thyme
1tsp	salt
1	lemon
2	eggs

Cut the chicken or turkey into serving pieces. In a large pot heat the lard or oil (or a combination of the two). Fry the almonds, bread and peeled garlic. Remove to a blender or processor. Add the saffron, peppercorns, nutmeg, cloves and parsley and process to make a smooth paste, adding the wine or sherry. In the fat in the pot brown the pieces of chicken with the diced ham. Add the almond paste, remaining wine, stock, bay, thyme and salt. Cover and simmer until chicken is very tender, about 40 minutes. Remove the chicken to a serving bowl. Beat the eggs with the lemon juice and stir into the sauce in the pot. Cook on a low heat, stirring, until sauce is thickened. Add more stock if necessary to make a sauce the consistency of thick cream. Pour over the chicken and garnish with chopped parsley. Serves 6 to 8.

POLLO EN SAMFAINA A LA CATALANA
Catalan Chicken With Summer Vegetables

1	chicken, jointed
100ml | 3 1/2fl oz	oil or lard
2	onions, sliced
3	cloves garlic, chopped
2	tomatoes, peeled and chopped
75ml |2 1/2fl oz	white wine
	salt and pepper
	bay, thyme, parsley
1	large aubergine, peeled and diced
2	green peppers, cut in squares
1	medium courgette, diced

Rub the chicken pieces with salt and pepper. Heat half the oil or lard in a pot or deep casserole and brown the chicken pieces on all sides. When partially browned, add the sliced onions and garlic. Then add the chopped tomatoes, wine, salt and pepper, bay, thyme and parsley. Cook the chicken on a medium heat. While chicken is cooking, heat the remaining oil in a frying pan and sauté the diced aubergine, peppers and courgette. Add to the chicken during the last 15 minutes of cooking. Serves 4 to 6.

POLLO AL JEREZ
Chicken With Sherry

1	chicken, jointed
4tbsp	olive oil
100g | 3 1/2oz	ham or bacon, diced
1	onion, chopped
150g | 5oz	mushrooms, sliced
150ml | 1/4pt	dry sherry
1	bay-leaf
	salt and pepper

Heat the oil in a pot or casserole and brown the chicken pieces. Add the diced ham, chopped onion and sliced mushrooms and sauté for 5 minutes. Pour in the sherry, add bay-leaf and season with salt and pepper. Cover and simmer until chicken is very tender, about 20 minutes. Serves 4 to 6.

Variation: Substitute medium-sweet *oloroso* sherry or Málaga wine for the dry sherry. Finish off with a little cream.

POLLO AL CHILINDRON
Chicken With Red Peppers

1	chicken, jointed
	salt and pepper
4	red bell peppers
4tbsp	oil
4	cloves garlic, chopped
200g | 7oz	ham, diced
1	onion, finely chopped
3	large tomatoes, peeled and chopped

Rub the chicken pieces with salt and pepper and set aside. Roast the peppers under the grill or spear them and hold over gas flame, turning them, until blistered and charred. Remove and let them sit, covered with a cloth until cool. Then peel them. Cut the flesh into wide strips. Heat the oil in a pot or casserole and brown the chicken pieces in it. Add the garlic, ham and onion. Fry for a few minutes, then add the strips of pepper and the tomatoes. Cook the chicken until very tender, about 25 minutes. The sauce should be fairly thick. Serves 4 to 6

PECHUGA DE POLLO A LA PLANCHA CON SALSA DE ACEITUNAS
Grilled Chicken Breast With Olive Sauce

4	chicken breasts, boned
75g | 2 1/2oz	green olives, pitted
1tbsp	finely chopped onion
1	clove garlic, minced
2tbsp	parsley, chopped
1/2tsp	paprika
4tbsp	olive oil
2tsp	vinegar
	salt and pepper

Split the chicken breasts and flatten the halves slightly. Brush them with olive oil and cook on a hot griddle until done, about 3 minutes on each side. Remove to a serving platter. Chop the olives and mix in a bowl with the chopped onion, garlic, parsley, paprika, remaining oil, vinegar, salt and pepper. Spoon the sauce over the grilled chicken. Serve hot or cold. Serves 4.

PAVO RELLENO
Stuffed Turkey

1	turkey, 4-5kg | 9-11lb
50g | 2oz	lard
250g | 9oz	pork or ham, chopped
200g | 7oz	fresh pork sausages
50g | 2oz	prunes, pitted and soaked
50g | 2oz	dried apricots, soaked
25g | 1oz	Málaga raisins, seeded
2	apples, peeled and cored
25g | 1oz	pine-nuts
10	chestnuts, roasted and peeled
1/2tsp	cinnamon
	salt and pepper
50g | 2oz	breadcrumbs
100ml | 3 1/2fl oz	sherry
	sliced pork fat for barding
	thyme, oregano, bay, rosemary

Clean the turkey and rub it inside and out with salt and a little of the sherry. Heat the lard in a large pan and in it sauté the turkey liver until browned on all sides. Remove and chop it. To the fat add the chopped pork or ham and the sausages, cut into pieces. Chop the prunes, apricots, and apples, and add to the pan with the chopped liver, raisins, pine-nuts, chestnuts, cinnamon, salt and pepper and breadcrumbs. Stir in the sherry and cook for a few minutes until liquid is absorbed. Stuff the turkey with this mixture. Sew up the openings. Cover the breast with thinly sliced pork fat and truss the bird with string, tying legs and wings close to the body. Put the turkey in a roasting pan with a bouquet garni of herbs. Put in a very hot oven for 10 minutes, then reduce heat to moderate and roast the bird, basting frequently. After an hour's roasting, add a glassful of wine and continue adding wine as it is cooked away. Allow about 22 minutes per 1/2 kilo | 1lb of turkey (unstuffed weight). Remove pork fat from turkey during last 30 minutes of roasting to allow breast to brown. Place turkey on a serving platter and let it sit 10 minutes before carving. De-grease the pan juices and serve with the turkey.

Variation: Chicken, goose or capon can be prepared in the same manner. Adjust quantities for a smaller fowl.

PATO A LA SEVILLANA
Seville-Style Duck

The finest olives, of course, come from Seville.

2	ducklings, each about 2kg	4 1/2lb
75ml	2 1/2fl oz	oil
1	onion, sliced
1tbsp	flour
1/2litre	1pt	white wine
1	lemon
1	sprig parsley
1	bay-leaf
2	carrots, peeled and quartered
	salt and pepper
	water or stock
150g	5oz	olives, pitted and chopped

Cut the ducks into quarters. Heat the oil in a large pot or

casserole and brown the pieces of duck in it with the sliced onion. Remove the duck when browned and pour off excess fat. Stir the flour into the drippings. Let it begin to brown, then add the wine. Return the duck to the casserole with the quartered lemon, parsley, bay-leaf, carrots, salt and pepper. Add enough water or stock to nearly cover the duck. Cover the casserole and cook until the duck is fork tender, about 1 1/2 hours. Remove duck to a serving dish. Skim fat from sauce, then strain it and return to the pot with the chopped olives. Cook 10 minutes and pour over the duck. Serves 6.

PERDICES EN ESCABECHE
Marinated Partridge

4	partridges
75ml | 2 1/2fl oz	olive oil
8	tiny onions
3	cloves garlic, crushed
2	carrots, peeled
3	bay-leaves
1tsp	thyme
1tsp	oregano
1tsp	paprika
10	peppercorns
3	cloves
1tsp	salt
100ml | 3 1/2 fl oz	white wine
100ml | 3 1/2 fl oz	vinegar
200ml | 7fl oz	water
1	lemon, sliced
	parsley

Clean the partridges and rub them inside and out with salt and pepper. Truss them with string so they keep their shape. Heat the oil in a frying pan and slowly brown them, one or two at a time. When golden, transfer them to a casserole. Peel the onions and cut a slit in the stem ends and add to the oil with the crushed garlic and carrots, halved lengthwise. Then add the bay, thyme, oregano, paprika, peppercorns, cloves, salt and white wine. Pour this over the partridges in the casserole and add the vinegar and water. Bring to the boil, then cover and cook very slowly until the birds are tender, about 40 minutes.

Remove from heat and let them cool in the liquid. Remove the partridges and discard the string. Place them in a glass or crockery bowl. Strain the cooking liquid and pour it over the partridges, which should be completely immersed. Slice the carrots and add them and the onions to the bowl. Cover tightly and chill for at least 2 days. Serve at room temperature or reheat very gently. Garnish with sliced lemon and parsley. One partridge serves 1 person as a main course; 2 as a starter.

CONEJO EN SALSA DE ALMENDRAS
Rabbit in Almond Sauce

1	rabbit, about 1 1/2kg | 3 1/2lb
4tbsp	oil
5	cloves garlic
20	almonds, blanched and skinned
1/4tsp	cinnamon
1tbsp	chopped parsley
10	peppercorns
2	cloves
1/2tsp	saffron
1tsp	salt
1	onion, chopped
50ml | 2fl oz	water
1/4litre | 1/2pt	white wine
2	bay-leaves

Cut the rabbit into serving pieces and rub them with salt and pepper. Set aside the liver. Heat the oil in a pot or casserole and fry 4 cloves of the garlic and the almonds with the rabbit liver until they are browned. Remove them to a blender or processor and add the cinnamon, parsley, peppercorns, cloves, saffron and salt. Process until smooth, adding a little of the water to make a smooth paste. In the same oil brown the pieces of rabbit, adding the chopped onion. Add the almond paste to the rabbit with the remaining water, wine and bay-leaves. Cover and simmer until very tender, about 45 minutes, adding more liquid if needed. Serves 4 to 6.

Variation: Chicken is prepared in the same manner.

CONEJO TARRACONENSE
Tarragona-Style Rabbit

1	rabbit, about 2kg |4 1/2lb
100ml	3 1/2fl oz	oil
1	onion, chopped
4	tomatoes, peeled and chopped
150ml	1/4pt	red wine
	bay, thyme, parsley, rosemary
	salt and pepper
	grated nutmeg
1/2tsp	saffron
1	chilli pepper or cayenne
2	cloves garlic
20g	3/4oz	dark chocolate
1tbsp	flour

Cut the rabbit into serving pieces. Heat the oil in a pot or casserole and slowly brown the rabbit pieces and the liver. Remove the liver and reserve it. Add the chopped onion to the rabbit and continue frying. Then add the tomatoes, the wine, herbs, salt and pepper and nutmeg. Cover the pan and let the rabbit cook very slowly. In a blender grind the saffron, fried liver, chilli pepper, garlic and chocolate. Toast the flour in a small pan over a medium heat, stirring until it is slightly coloured. Add to the blender with about 100ml | 3 1/2fl oz hot water to make a smooth paste. Add this mixture to the rabbit and continue cooking until rabbit is very tender, about 1 3/4 hours total. Serve with boiled new potatoes and garnish with chopped parsley. Serves 4 to 6.

MEAT

Meat in Spain is generally good. Pork *(cerdo)* is the best. It is raised from one end of the country to the other and consumed from jowl to tail, fresh and cured, in hundreds of different preparations. In central Spain where sheep are raised, lamb dishes are renowned. Baby lamb *(cordero)* is roasted in wood-fired bakers' ovens or stewed in great cauldrons to make sustaining shepherds' dishes. Baby kid *(cabrito)* is also a popular dish in Spain, where goats — even today an important source of milk — graze on rocky hillsides.

Beef and dairy cattle once thrived only in the wet northern regions of Spain where excellent grazing lands could sustain them. Thus, Asturias and Galicia even evolved a "butter" cuisine. Enormous beef chops are consumed with gusto there — though the rest of the country has discovered this carnivore's dream as well. Modern feed crops have made it possible to raise good beef in Spain. However, it is generally slaughtered younger than in other countries. *Ternera* translates as veal, but really means young beef. Milk-fed veal is called *ternera lechal* or *ternera de Avila*. Real "beefy" beef is *buey*.

Good cuts of quality meat, whether beef, pork or lamb, are usually very simply grilled or roasted, possibly strewn with garlic, and paired with a heap of chips. Sauces such as *alioli* or the following blue cheese sauce are good accompaniments.

CHULETON CON SALSA DE CABRALES
Beef Chop With Blue Cheese Sauce

Cabrales is a blue cheese made from cows' milk in Cabrales (Asturias).

4	beef rib chops, thickly cut
100ml | 3 1/2fl oz	oil
	freshly ground black pepper
5	cloves garlic, chopped
3tbsp	chopped parsley
200g | 7oz	blue cheese
60g | 2oz	butter, softened
1tbsp	minced onion
6tbsp	white wine or dry cider

Trim fat from chops (entrecote or other steak can be substituted) and put them on a platter. Drizzle with the oil and sprinkle with pepper, chopped garlic and parsley. Let them sit for an hour, turning several times. Prepare charcoal. Meanwhile place blue cheese, butter, onion and wine or cider in blender or processor container and whirl until smooth. Sauce should be thick and creamy — add additional liquid as needed. Grill the steaks over hot coals or on a hot griddle and serve topped with the sauce. Serves 4.

FILETES DE TERNERA EMPANADOS
Breaded Veal Cutlets

4	veal cutlets
5	cloves garlic, chopped
2tbsp	chopped parsley
1/2tsp	salt
2	lemons
1	egg, beaten
50g | 2oz	fine breadcrumbs
	pinch of thyme
60ml | 2fl oz	olive oil
	parsley

Place each cutlet between cling film and pound thin. Cut them in half if they are very large. Place on a plate and sprinkle with the chopped garlic, parsley, salt and juice of 1 lemon. Set aside for 30 minutes, turning the meat once. Place the beaten egg in a shallow bowl, the breadcrumbs mixed with the thyme in another. Dip the cutlets first in egg then dredge in breadcrumbs and fry in olive oil until browned on both sides. Serve with lemon wedges and parsley.

Variation: Prepare pork cutlets in the same manner.

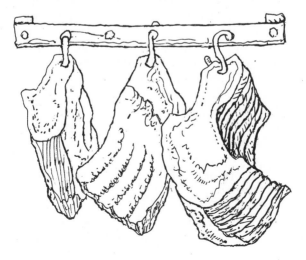

TERNERA MECHADA
Pot Roast

1 1/2kg | 3 1/2lb	boneless beef roast (such as round)
5	peppercorns
1	clove
	grating of fresh nutmeg
2tbsp	chopped parsley
2	cloves garlic
1	hard-cooked egg
1tbsp	oil
50g | 2oz	salt pork in thin strips
4tbsp	lard or oil
1	onion, quartered
3	carrots, peeled and halved
2	tomatoes, quartered
1	head garlic, roasted
1	bay-leaf
100ml | 3 1/2fl oz	sherry
150ml | 1/4pt	beef stock or water
1tsp	salt

Roll the meat into a uniform shape and tie it with twine. Grind together the peppercorns, clove, nutmeg, parsley, garlic, egg and oil to make a paste. Cut the salt pork into thin slivers. With a sharp knife, cut deep gashes into the meat and with the knife blade insert some of the paste and a piece of salt pork. Continue, spacing the gashes regularly on the meat's surface. Heat the lard in a pot big enough to hold the piece of meat and brown it very slowly on all sides. Add the quartered onion, carrot, tomatoes and roasted garlic cloves. (To roast garlic, spear the whole head on a fork and hold it over a gas flame or place under grill, turning, until it is blackened and charred. Peel off the skin and add the whole cloves to the pot.) Put in the bay-leaf, sherry and stock and cook the meat very slowly until fork tender, about 2 hours, adding more stock as needed. Remove the meat to a serving platter, discard the string and slice it. Sieve the sauce and spoon it over the meat. Serve with potato purée or potatoes which have been browned in lard with a little garlic. Serves 8.

Variation: TERNERA AL PEBRE, peppery pot roast. Add 1/2tsp coarsely ground pepper and 1/2tsp ground cumin to the meat sauce. Use the same preparation for pork and lamb roast.

ESTOFADO DE BUEY
Beef Stew

1kg | 2lb	stewing beef
1	green pepper
1	large tomato, peeled
2	onions, sliced
2	carrots, halved lengthwise
1/2tsp	saffron
8	peppercorns
2	cloves
1/4tsp	cinnamon
1	head garlic, roasted
100ml | 3 1/2fl oz	water
50ml | 2fl oz	oil
2	bay-leaves
2tsp	salt
1/4litre | 1/2pt	white wine
5	potatoes, peeled

Cut the meat into cubes. Place in a stew pot with the green pepper, cut in strips, the tomato cut in quarters, the onions and carrots. Crush the saffron, peppercorns, cloves, cinnamon and dissolve in the water. Add to the meat with the cloves of roasted garlic. (To roast garlic, see previous recipe.) Add the oil, bay-leaves, parsley, salt and white wine. Cover and cook for 1 hour, adding more water or stock as needed to keep the meat just covered with liquid. Then add the potatoes and cook another 30 minutes. Other vegetables — broad beans, peas, pumpkin — can be added to this stew. Sliced pears or apples can be added at the end of cooking time. Serves 6.

GUISO CON ALCACHOFAS
Beef Stew With Artichokes

1/2kg | 1lb	stewing beef
3tbsp	oil
7	cloves garlic
450g | 1lb	fresh peas
6	fresh artichokes
2tbsp	chopped parsley
2	onions, quartered
2	bay-leaves
2	cloves
10	peppercorns
1/4tsp	saffron
1tsp	salt
600ml | 1pt	stock or water
85ml | 3fl oz	white wine
5	medium potatoes

Cut the beef into cubes. Brown it in hot oil in a large pot or casserole with the whole, peeled garlic cloves. Shell the peas. Remove outer leaves from artichokes, slice off top two-thirds, and cut them in half. Blanch them in boiling water for 5 minutes. Add peas and artichokes to pot with the parsley, onions and bay-leaves. Crush the cloves, pepper, saffron and salt and add to the stew with the stock or water and wine. Cover and cook until meat is nearly tender, about 1 hour. Peel the potatoes, cut in chunks, and add to the stew. Cook another 40 minutes. Serves 4.

Tip: Use frozen peas and artichoke hearts for this stew, adding them with the potatoes.

RABO DE TORO GUISADO
Braised Oxtail

1	oxtail, about 1 1/4kg | 2 3/4lb
4tbsp	oil
1	onion, chopped
1	leek, chopped
3	carrots, chopped
2	cloves garlic, chopped
50g | 2oz	ham, diced
75ml | 2 1/2fl oz	brandy
100ml | 3 1/2fl oz	red wine or sherry

bay-leaf, parsley, thyme
salt and pepper
dash of cloves
1   piece chilli pepper or cayenne
1   tomato, peeled and chopped

Have the butcher cut the tail into segments of about 7cm |
2 3/4in. Parboil them in boiling water and drain. In a pot heat
the oil and add the chopped onion, leek, carrots, garlic and
ham. Sauté until softened, then add the blanched pieces of
oxtail and sauté on a high heat. Add the brandy, set it alight,
and stir with a long-handled spoon until flames subside. Then
add the red wine or sherry, the herbs and spices, the chilli and
chopped tomato. Simmer until the meat is very tender, about
2 hours, adding stock or water as needed. When cooked, the
sauce should be fairly thick from reduction. If not, thicken it
with a little flour mixed in water. Serves 4.

LOMO EN ADOBO
Marinated Pork Loin

3/4kg	1 3/4lb	boned pork loin
4	cloves garlic
1tsp	oregano
	pinch of thyme and rosemary
1/4tsp	saffron
10	peppercorns
1/2tsp	salt
1tsp	paprika
150ml	1/4pt	vinegar
2tbsp	oil

Put the pork loin in a deep bowl. Crush the garlic with the
oregano, thyme, rosemary, saffron, peppercorns, salt and
paprika. Dissolve the paste in a little of the vinegar. Pour over
the meat with the rest of the vinegar. Cover and marinate,
refrigerated, for about 48 hours, turning the meat 2 or 3 times
a day. Then drain the piece of meat and pat it dry. Place it in
an oiled oven tin and rub with the oil. Place in a very hot oven
for 5 minutes, then reduce heat to moderate and roast the pork
until done, about 40 minutes, basting with the pan drippings.
Slice and serve. Serves 6. Instead of roasting, the pork loin can
be thinly sliced and the slices fried in oil.

SOLOMILLO DE CERDO AL JEREZ
Pork Fillet With Sherry

2	pork fillets (about 650g | 1lb 6 oz)
50g | 2oz	*serrano* ham or lean bacon
2tbsp	lard
1	head garlic
1-2	dozen small onions
100ml | 3 1/2fl oz	dry sherry
	thyme and parsley

Lard the fillets with strips of ham or lay strips of ham over the narrow end of the fillets and double them over, securing with string. Melt the lard in a frying pan and place the fillets in it, turning to brown on all sides. Add the peeled garlic, peeled onions, sherry, thyme and parsley. Simmer until the meat is cooked, about 30 minutes. Slice the fillets and serve with the pan juices, onions and garlic. Serves 4.

COCHINILLO ASADO
Roast Suckling Pig

One of the glories of Castile, where baby pig is roasted in wood-fired brick ovens.

1	whole pig, 3-4 weeks, weighing 3 1/2-4kg | 7 1/2-9lb
100g | 3 1/2oz	lard
4	cloves garlic
	bay-leaves, thyme, rosemary
1tbsp	salt
1tbsp	vinegar
6tbsp	water

Buy an oven-ready suckling pig and have the butcher open it lengthwise without cutting through the backbone. (If oven size is a consideration, have the pig cut in quarters.) Preheat oven to hot — 200 ºC/400 ºF. Beat the lard until softened and add the crushed garlic. Wrap the ears and feet in foil to keep them from browning too fast. Place the pig, skin side down in a roasting pan and spread the meat with half the lard. Sprinkle with a little crushed bay, thyme and rosemary. Add enough hot water to cover the bottom of the roasting pan in order to prevent the skin from sticking. Place in the preheated oven and immediately turn down the heat to medium. Roast the pig for 1 hour, adding additional water if needed. Remove from oven and carefully turn the meat skin side up. With a fork or knitting needle, prick the skin all over and brush with remaining lard. Return to oven for 15 minutes. Then mix the salt, vinegar and water and baste the meat with it. Roast, basting frequently, until skin is crackly and meat is done, about 30 minutes more, raising heat if necessary.

Variation: Roast baby lamb, *lechazo,* in the same way.

MAGRO CON TOMATE
Pork With Tomato

1/2kg | 1lb	pork, cut in cubes
4tbsp	oil
1	onion, finely chopped
2	cloves garlic, chopped
1kg | 2lb	tomatoes, peeled and chopped
2tsp	salt
1	bay-leaf

Fry the pork cubes in oil until browned. Add the chopped onion and garlic and fry a few minutes, then the chopped tomatoes. Season with salt and add bay-leaf. Simmer until pork is very tender and tomatoes reduced to a thick sauce, about 30 minutes. Serves 4.

CHULETAS DE CORDERO A LA BATURRA
Aragon Style Lamb Chops

3/4kg | 1 3/4lb	lamb chops
4tbsp	oil or lard
1	onion, chopped
3	cloves garlic, chopped
150g | 5oz	ham, diced
1tsp salt 5	tomatoes, peeled and chopped

Heat the oil or lard in a frying pan and brown the lamb chops on both sides. Transfer them to a casserole. In the same fat, sauté the chopped onion, garlic and diced ham for a few minutes. Add the chopped tomatoes and fry for several minutes. Season with salt and pour over the lamb chops. Cover and cook them until tender, about 30 minutes. Serve in the same casserole.

Variation: CHULETAS DE CORDERO A LA PAM-PLONA, Pamplona-style lamb chops. Add sliced chorizo to the casserole with the tomato sauce. Simmer or bake until chops are tender.

CORDERO A LA MIEL
Lamb With Honey

1	leg of lamb, weighing about 1 3/4kg |3 3/4lb
75ml | 2 1/2fl oz	olive oil
1	large onion, thinly sliced
3	small green peppers, shredded
2	cloves garlic, chopped
1	slice lemon
3tbsp	brandy
115ml | 4fl oz	white wine
1/2tsp	saffron
1tbsp	paprika
1/4tsp	ground pepper
	pinch of cinnamon
	salt
50ml | 2fl oz	wine vinegar
85g | 3oz	honey

Have the butcher bone the leg of lamb and cut it into thick pieces. Heat the oil in a pot and sauté the sliced onion, thinly sliced green peppers and the garlic. Add the pieces of lamb and brown them. Shred the lemon, peel and all, and add to the lamb with the brandy and wine. Crush the saffron with the paprika, pepper, cinnamon and salt and add to the meat. Cook, covered, until the meat is very tender, about 1 hour. When meat is done, add the vinegar and honey and cook 10 minutes more. Serves 6.

CAZUELA CAMPESINA
Country Casserole of Lamb

1 1/2kg | 3 1/2lb	baby lamb (or lamb chops)
150ml | 1/4pt	oil

8	medium potatoes, peeled and sliced
6	medium tomatoes, sliced
2	onions, sliced
2	green peppers, cut in strips
3tbsp	chopped parsley
1	head garlic, roasted
4	bay-leaves
2tsp	salt
2	cloves garlic
10	peppercorns
2	cloves
1tsp	cinnamon
1tsp	saffron
1/2litre | 1pt	white wine

Have the butcher cut the lamb into even-sized pieces. Pour the oil into a large roasting pan or deep casserole. Put a layer of sliced potatoes on the bottom and alternate with layers of sliced tomatoes and onions. Put in the meat. Cover with strips of green pepper, chopped parsley, cloves of roasted garlic (to roast garlic, spear it with a fork and hold over gas flame or put under grill, turning, until it is blackened and charred, then peel), bay-leaves and another layer of sliced potatoes, tomatoes and onion. Crush together the salt, 2 cloves of garlic, peppercorns, cloves, cinnamon and saffron. Dissolve in a little white wine and add to the casserole with the rest of the wine. Put the casserole in a hot oven for 10 minutes, then reduce the heat to moderate and cook until meat and potatoes are very tender, about 2 hours. Serves 8.

CALDERETA DE CORDERO
Lamb Stew

1kg | 2lb	boned lamb shoulder
1	onion, quartered
2	tomatoes, quartered
2	green peppers, cut in half
1	head garlic, roasted
	bay-leaf, parsley, thyme
1/2tsp	salt
50ml | 2fl oz	oil
8	peppercorns
1	clove
1tsp	paprika
1/2tsp	cumin
1	slice bread, soaked in water
	fresh mint leaves

Cut the lamb into cubes and put in a pot or casserole. Add enough water to just cover the meat. Bring to the boil, skim the froth and reduce to a simmer. Add the onion, tomatoes, peppers, roasted garlic (to roast garlic, see previous recipe), bouquet of herbs, salt and oil. Crush the peppercorns, clove, paprika, cumin and mix with the soaked bread to make a paste and add to the pot. Cover and simmer until meat is very tender, about 45 minutes. Garnish with finely chopped mint leaves. Serves 6 to 8.

CABRITO AL AJO CABELLIN
Baby Lamb or Kid Fried With Garlic

Look for this speciality in the country restaurants around Granada and the Sierra Nevada.

1 1/2kg | 3 1/2lb	baby lamb or kid (or substitute lamb chops)
1	lamb's liver or 150g | 5oz chicken livers
75ml | 2 1/2fl oz	oil
1	head garlic (about 10 cloves)
1	slice bread
10	peppercorns
1tsp	oregano
	pinch of cayenne
2tsp	paprika

1tsp	salt
1tbsp	vinegar
2	bay-leaves
1/2litre | 1pt	white wine

Have the lamb or kid cut into evenly-sized pieces. Cut the liver into several pieces. Heat the oil in a frying pan and sauté the liver until lightly browned and remove it. In the same oil fry 5 cloves of garlic and the bread until browned, and remove. Add the pieces of lamb to the oil and continue turning it until browned. In the blender or processor grind the peppercorns, oregano, cayenne, paprika, salt and 2 cloves of garlic with the fried garlic, bread and liver. Add the vinegar and a little wine to make a smooth paste. Stir into the meat and add the remaining wine and bay-leaves. Cover and simmer until meat is very tender, about 1 hour. Serves 8.

COSTILLAS DE CORDERO A LA BRASA
Barbecued Lamb Ribs

2	racks of lamb riblets
1tsp	salt
3tbsp	chopped parsley
1tsp	oregano
1tsp	thyme
1	bay-leaf
	freshly ground pepper
1	lemon
3tbsp	oil
	alioli sauce (see recipe, page 21)

Have the butcher cut the racks into sections of 3 ribs. Place them in a large bowl. Mix the salt, parsley, oregano, thyme, bay, pepper, juice of the lemon and oil with a few spoonfuls of water. Pour over the lamb ribs and marinate for 4 hours or, refrigerated, overnight. Barbecue the ribs over hot coals, basting with the marinade, until they are browned, about 10 minutes per side. Serve accompanied by the alioli sauce. Serves 4 to 6.

SEAFOOD DISHES

WITH NEARLY 4,000 MILES of coastline, it's not surprising that many of Spain's best dishes consist of fish and shellfish. Spaniards eat more fish than any other Europeans and they're willing to pay more for it than they do for meat. Gorgeous gilt-head bream, glistening sea bass or huge prawns cost nearly double the price of excellent entrecote or leg of lamb. However, inexpensive blue fish — sardines, fresh anchovies, mackerel, tuna and bonito — are also popular, so there are inspired ways to cook them. Additionally, seafood soups and stews make delicious use of small but tasty specimens.

Spanish cooks have a knowing way with fish. Firm-fleshed fish stand up to grilling and braising; flaky ones get floured and lightly fried. Bland fish take to rich sauces and strongly flavoured ones to marinades and spices. So, in Spain, each fish has its favoured manner of cooking. Though you might not find all of these fish in your local market — some really are at home only in the Mediterranean — similar ones can be successfully substituted in the following recipes. To give you an idea of the range of fish in Spanish waters, following is a listing of some of the favourites.

Hake *(merluza)*: Lean and flaky, possibly Spain's favourite fish. Perfect for fish and chips, but also lovely in green sauce in the Basque style. Be careful not to overcook. Hake belongs to the cod family, so if not available, substitute cod, haddock, coley, whiting, pollack, forkbeard, ling.

Blue fish: From the tiny fresh anchovy, *boquerón,* to the huge tuna, *atún,* blue fish are a delicious bargain. Higher in fat content than most fish, they stay moist and tender. They must all be absolutely fresh. Grill, braise in a flavourful sauce, or bake. Between the tiny and the huge are sardines, *sardinas; horse mackerel, jurel;* mackerel, *caballa;* pompano, *palometa;* amberjack, *pez limón;* bonito. Use them interchangeably. Substitute as for size, thus, smelt for achovy; herring for sardine; swordfish for tuna; bluefish for amberjack; salmon for bonito; trout for pompano.

Bream or, in American waters, porgy: This includes Spain's runner-up for favourite fish, the *besugo,* red bream, as well as the esteemed gilt-head, *dorada,* and other popular breams such as the *pargo, urta* and *sargo.* They are all fine-flavoured, firm and moist in texture. Any bream can be substituted, or use instead redfish or snapper.

Rockfish: These firm-fleshed fish are classic for Mediterranean fish soups. Large specimens can be baked or grilled. Finest is the *gallineta,* blue-mouth or "Norway haddock." Others are the scorpion-fish such as *cabracho* and *rascacio;* the gurnards, including *rubio;* the weevers, such as *araña.* Redfish or bream would make good substitutes or, for soups, meaty fish such as angler or conger.

Flat fish: In Spain as in Britain, the sole, *lenguado,* is the finest in this category. Also to be had are turbot, *rodaballo;* plaice or flounder, *platija;* angler or monkfish, *rape;* and John Dory, *pez de San Pedro.*

Mullet: The red mullet, *salmonete,* is the Mediterranean "signature" fish. It makes fabulous eating, simply grilled, sprinkled with herbs. There really is no substitute in flavour, though redfish, snapper or red bream make pretty alternatives.

Sea bass, *lubina:* A superb fish, with a buttery texture and clean taste. Good poached, grilled, steamed, or baked. Its close relatives *baila* and *cherna* are less expensive. Grouper, *mero,* is excellent white fish too. Croaker or meagre, *corvina,* or grey mullet, *lisa,* could be substituted for any of them.

Tip: Very fresh fish profits from being salted and left to sit for 15-30 minutes before cooking to eliminate excess liquid and firm-up flesh. Frozen fish should not be salted or it will be dry. Let it thaw slowly in the refrigerator or, if it is to be cooked in a sauce, cook it without defrosting first, adding to cooking time accordingly. Fish to be deep-fried must, of course, be completely thawed before cooking.

BESUGO A LA ESPALDA
Grilled Bream "On Its Back"

This is traditionally cooked over charcoal — using a hinged grill to simplify turning the fish — and then boned. Easier:

open up the fish, remove the spine, and grill or bake each fillet, basting with olive oil. Allow a whole fish of at least 3/4kg l 1 3/4lb for 2 people.

While fish is grilling, gently heat 8 tablespoons olive oil with 6 cloves garlic, coarsley chopped, 4 tbsp chopped parsley, and 8 *very tiny* chilli peppers or 2 chillies, chopped. Remove from heat and add the juice of 1 lemon. Drizzle this mixture over 4 grilled fillets.

Variation: BESUGO A LA MADRILEÑA, Madrid-style bream. Add 3 tablespoons fine breadcrumbs to the oil and garlic mixture. Put the cleaned fish into a well-oiled pan and top with the crumb mixture and bake in a very hot oven. For a very large fish, add a little white wine to the pan.

PESCADO A LA SAL
Salt-Baked Fish

Try this at a beachside restaurant on the Costa Blanca or the Costa del Sol. The salt bakes into a crust, sealing in the fish juices. Crack the crust and peel it away with the skin. Spoon the flesh off the bones on to plates and serve accompanied by two or three sauces, such as *alioli* and *aliño* (use the preceding oil-garlic-parsley mixture, omitting the chilli). Use a large bream, especially gilt-head, or sea bass, snapper, or redfish for this dish.

If possible, have the fish drawn through the gills. Wash and dry well. Measure it at the thickest part and allow 15 minutes in a hot oven for every 2 cm l 3/4in, or about 20 minutes for a fish weighing 3/4kg l 1 3/4lb. Mix 2 tbsp of flour with 2 kg of coarse salt. Oil an oven pan and put in a layer of the salt. Place the fish on top and cover with the remaining salt. Place in a preheated hot oven and bake as indicated above. A fish of this weight serves 2-3 people.

PESCADO AL HORNO
Baked Fish

Best done with a large bream, weighing at least 1kg l 2lbs, but bass, rockfish, grouper or even fish fillets could be substituted. If using small fish or fillets, put the casserole with potatoes and vegetables to bake before adding the fish.

1kg | 2lb	whole fish (or larger)
100ml | 3 1/2fl oz	olive oil
1kg | 2lb	potatoes, thinly sliced
5	cloves garlic, chopped
3	tablespoons chopped parsley
2	green peppers, chopped
	salt and pepper
1	onion, sliced
2	tomatoes, sliced
100ml | 3 1/2fl oz	white wine
1	bay-leaf

Rub the fish inside and out with salt and let it sit 15 minutes. Pour the oil into the bottom of a heat-proof oven dish and add a layer of half the thinly sliced potatoes. Sprinkle half the chopped garlic and parsley and green pepper over them and season with salt and pepper. Then place a layer of the sliced onions and tomatoes. Add the rest of the potatoes, the remaining garlic, parsley and peppers and again sprinkle with salt and pepper. Lay the fish on top of the potatoes and top it with a few remaining slices of tomato. Put pieces of bay-leaf around it. Pour the wine over. Place the pan on a medium flame. When liquid begins to simmer, cover with foil and put the pan into a medium oven. Bake until potatoes are very tender, about 30 minutes, removing foil during last few minutes. Serves about 4 to 6, depending on size of fish.

URTA A LA ROTEÑA
Rota-Style Bream

A casseroled fish dish, well known from Seville to Cádiz. Redfish or snapper could be used instead of the bream.

1kg | 2lb	whole bream
	flour
115ml | 4fl oz	olive oil
50ml | 2fl oz	brandy
1	onion, chopped
2	bell peppers, cut in strips
1	large tomato
1/2tsp	thyme

	bay-leaf
	salt and pepper
50ml | 2fl oz	white wine

Cut the fish into crosswise slices, then cut each slice into two, removing the bone. Sprinkle lightly with salt and dredge in flour. Heat half the oil in a heat-proof casserole and brown the pieces of fish on both sides. Pour in the brandy, ignite it and gently swirl the casserole until flames subside. Meanwhile, in another pan, heat the remaining oil and sauté the chopped onion and peppers. Peel the tomato and purée in a blender, straining out the seeds. Add to the onion with the thyme, bay-leaf, salt and pepper and white wine. Simmer the sauce until reduced, about 15 minutes. Add to the fish, combine well, and simmer until the fish is done, about 10 minutes more. Serves 4.

MERLUZA A LA VASCA
Basque-Style Hake

4	hake steaks, each 200g | 7oz
75ml | 2 1/2fl oz	olive oil
6	cloves garlic, chopped
1 tbsp	flour
4 tbsp	chopped parsley
115ml | 4fl oz	white wine
250g | 9oz	clams, scrubbed and steamed
50g | 2oz	cooked peas
1 dozen	cooked asparagus tips
1	hard-cooked egg

Salt the fish steaks and set aside for 15 minutes. Heat the oil in an earthenware casserole and add the coarsely chopped garlic. Let stew for a few minutes, then add the fish steaks. Turn them after a few minutes — they don't actually brown. Cook another 3 minutes and sprinkle with the flour and the chopped parsley. Add the wine. Then add the clams which have been steamed open, the cooked peas, cooked asparagus and quartered egg. Rock the casserole back and forth to amalgamate the sauce. Serve in the same casserole. Serves 4.

Variation: MERLUZA A LA SIDRA, hake with cider. Prepare the above recipe, omitting the peas, clams, asparagus and egg. Add 10 tbsp cider and continue swirling the pan. This is also a fine way to prepare steaks of sea bass or salmon.

MARMITAKO
Basque Tuna and Potato Casserole

1kg | 2lb	fresh tuna, bonito or mackerel
4tbsp	olive oil
1	onion, chopped
4	cloves garlic, chopped
2	green peppers, chopped
2	large tomatoes, chopped
1tsp	paprika
	pinch of cayenne
	salt and pepper
1kg | 2lb	potatoes
200ml | 7fl oz	white wine

Cut the fish into chunks, discarding the bone. Heat the oil in a heat-proof (earthenware) casserole and in it sauté the chopped onions, garlic, peppers and tomatoes until vegetables are softened. Add the paprika, cayenne, salt and pepper and cook until slightly reduced, about 5 minutes. Add the potatoes, peeled and cut in dice. Then add the wine. Cover and cook on a medium heat until potatoes are nearly tender. Then add the chunks of fish and additional water and cook until fish is done, about 15 minutes. The casserole should be fairly saucy. Remove from heat and let sit 5 minutes or more before serving. Serves 6.

FRITURA MALAGUEÑA
Málaga-Style Fish Fry

An Andalusian fish fry is the epitome of fried fish — the fish so fresh, the oil just crackling, the timing just right. For this wonderful platter, renowned from Málaga to Cádiz, allow per person a very small sole or a fillet; a slice of fresh hake; 5 or 6 rings of squid *(calamares);* 6-8 fresh anchovies *(boquerones);* 3 peeled prawns. Teeny-tiny *chanquetes* used to be included in this fish fry, but their capture is forbidden these days, in order to protect the young of other species. Refuse to eat them!

Wash and pat dry the pieces of fish. Dredge them in flour,

then shake off excess. (Andalusians use a special, square-framed sieve for shaking down fish.) Heat olive oil to almost smoking. It should be deep enough to cover the fish. Add the fish to the oil. Use a skimmer to remove fried fish as it turns golden. Sprinkle with salt. Serve all the fried fish on a big platter with wedges of lemon. Certainly, you can substitute cheaper oil. But try it at least once with real olive oil. You might be surprised at what a "light" fry it gives you.

PESCADO EN AMARILLO
Fish in Saffron Sauce

Use grey mullet, skate, anglerfish, bass, swordfish or any solid-fleshed fish.

1/2kg | 1lb	fish fillets or slices
	salt
	lemon
4tbsp	oil
1	slice bread, crusts removed
2	cloves garlic
1	small onion, chopped
1/2tsp	saffron
1tbsp	chopped parsley
1/4tsp	cumin
6tbsp	dry white wine

Salt the pieces of fish and sprinkle with lemon juice and let them sit for 15 minutes. Heat the oil in a frying pan and in it fry the bread and garlic just until lightly toasted, and remove. Add the chopped onion to the pan and fry until softened. Place the bread, garlic, onion and oil from the pan in blender with the saffron, parsley and wine. Blend to a smooth sauce. Arrange the fish in the same pan and pour the sauce over. Put on a moderate heat until sauce begins to simmer, then cover and cook until fish flakes, about 10 minutes for fillets. If sauce seems too thick, add a little water. Serve with lemon slices and a sprinkling of parsley. Serves 4.

Variation: SAFFRON FISH STEW. Cut potatoes into chunks and place them in a pot. Add just enough flavourful stock to cover them and cook until nearly tender. Add the fish and the saffron sauce and continue cooking until fish is done.

PESCADO EN SALSA DE ALMENDRAS
Fish in Almond Sauce

Anglerfish *(rape)* is especially good prepared in this manner. Use the head and trimmings to make fish stock.

3/4kg | 1 3/4lb	angler fish fillets or slices
4tbsp	oil
	flour
30	blanched almonds
2	cloves garlic
1	slice bread, crusts removed
1/2tsp	saffron
4tbsp	white wine or fish stock
1	medium onion, chopped
1	medium tomato, peeled and chopped
100ml | 3 1/2fl oz	fish stock or water
	salt and pepper
	parsley

Cut the fish into chunks, salt it and let it sit 15 minutes. Heat the oil and quickly brown the fish on both sides. Remove and set aside. In the same oil, fry the almonds, garlic and bread until golden, and remove. Place in blender with the saffron and white wine and whirl until smooth. In the same oil, fry the chopped onions until softened, then add the tomatoes and fry until slightly reduced. Add the almond paste and the fish stock. Season with salt and pepper. Return the pieces of fish to the pan and simmer until fish flakes easily, about 20 minutes. Garnish with parsley. Serves 6.

PESCADO EN PIMENTON
Paprika Fish

Use skate, angler, mullet, bass or other meaty fish or shellfish such as prawns.

3/4kg | 1 3/4lb	fish fillets or slices
75ml | 2 1/2fl oz	olive oil
6	cloves garlic
1tbsp	chopped parsley
1tsp	mild paprika
	dash of cayenne

1/4tsp	saffron
1tsp	oregano
2tsp	vinegar
	salt and pepper

Cut the fish into pieces. Heat the oil in a frying pan and fry the garlic and remove when golden. Add the pieces of fish to the pan and sauté on a hot fire. Crush the fried garlic in a mortar and mix with the parsley, paprika, cayenne, saffron, oregano, vinegar, and salt and pepper. Add this to the fish, cover and cook until fish flakes easily, about 15 minutes, adding a little water if needed. Serves 4.

PESCADO EN SALSA VERDE
Fish in Green Sauce

Use rockfish, redfish, rascasse, scorpion-fish, gurnard, snapper or bream.

3/4kg | 1 3/4lb	fish fillets or slices
6tbsp	olive oil
3	leeks, finely chopped
2	cloves garlic, chopped
4tbsp	chopped parsley
4	medium potatoes, thinly sliced
115ml | 4fl oz	water
	salt
	flour
175ml | 6fl oz	white wine
2tbsp	cooked peas

Salt the fish and set aside. In a casserole heat the oil and sauté the chopped leeks. Add the garlic, then the parsley and sliced potatoes. Cover with the water, add 2 tsp salt and bring to the boil. Simmer until potatoes are nearly tender, 25 minutes. Dredge the pieces of fish in flour and place them in the casserole. Pour in the wine. Cook until fish flakes easily, about 15 minutes. Don't stir the potatoes after adding the fish, but shake the casserole to prevent sticking. Garnish with cooked peas and serve from the same casserole. Serves 6.

PESCADO A LA MARINERA
Fish, Mariner's Style

Any white-fleshed fish will do nicely. Fish can be cut in crosswise slices or fillets. If using delicate fish such as hake, take care not to overcook.

1/2kg | 1lb	fish fillets or slices
6tbsp	olive oil
1	small onion, chopped
1	small green or red pepper, chopped
2	cloves garlic, chopped
3	small tomatoes, peeled and chopped
100ml | 3 1/2fl oz	white wine
	a few threads of saffron, crushed
	salt and pepper
	a few prawns
	a dozen clams
	parsley

Salt the fish and let it sit while preparing the sauce. Heat 3 tablespoons of the oil in a pan and sauté the chopped onion, pepper and garlic until softened. Add the chopped tomatoes and fry for a few minutes, then add the wine, saffron and salt and pepper. Cook on a medium heat until the sauce is reduced and thickened. In an earthenware or other heat-proof casserole, heat the remaining oil and sauté the pieces of fish, turning once. Add the prepared sauce to the casserole and simmer the fish (or place in a medium oven) until it flakes easily. Add the peeled prawns and scrubbed clams when fish is almost done, and cook until clam shells open. Serve, sprinkled with parsley, from the same casserole.

Variation: Turn this into a Mediterranean fish soup with the addition of stock. Serve over thick slices of bread which have been fried in oil with chopped garlic.

BROCHETA DE PESCADO
Fish Kebabs

Typical are swordfish, angler, fresh tuna, dogfish (a kind of shark) and prawns.

1/2kg | 1lb	swordfish steaks
2tbsp	oil
1tsp	salt
2tbsp	chopped parsley
	pinch of cumin
3	cloves garlic, chopped
1	lemon
1	tomato
1	onion
1	green pepper

Cut the fish into cubes about 4cm | 1 1/2in and place in a bowl. Add the oil, salt, parsley, cumin, chopped garlic and lemon juice. Leave to marinate for 30 minutes at room temperature, or longer refrigerated. Cut the tomato, onion and green pepper each into eighths. Thread the swordfish on to skewers, alternating with pieces of vegetable. Brush with marinade and cook over hot charcoal or on a griddle. Turn once and baste frequently with marinade until fish is done, about 8 minutes. Serve with *alioli,* garlic mayonnaise, or *salsa brava,* "fierce" sauce (see recipes in Chapter 1). Serves 4.

SALMONETES AL HORNO
CON HIERBAS
Red Mullet Baked With Herbs

4	red mullet, each weighing about 300g | 10oz
	sprigs of rosemary and thyme
4tbsp	olive oil
	lemon slices
2	tomatoes
2	cloves garlic, chopped
2tbsp	chopped parsley
4tbsp	fine breadcrumbs
150ml | 1/4pt	white wine

Gut the fish but leave whole. Salt lightly and let sit 15 minutes. Place a sprig of rosemary and thyme in the cavity of each one. Make two slashes almost to the bone in each and insert a thin half-slice of lemon in the slashes. Put 2 tablespoons of the oil in an oven dish and put in the fish. Slice the tomatoes and lay them over the fish. Sprinkle over the chopped garlic, parsley and breadcrumbs. Pour over the wine. Drizzle with the remaining oil. Bake in a preheated medium hot oven until fish flakes easily, about 20 minutes. Serve from the same oven dish. Bream can be prepared in the same manner.

SALMON A LA ASTURIANA
Salmon, Asturian Style

Asturias is known for its wild river salmon; the rest of Spain enjoys fresh farmed salmon imported from Norway.

4	salmon steaks
100g | 3 1/2oz	bacon or salt pork, diced
4tbsp	butter
	flour
150ml | 1/4pt	cider or *cava* (sparkling wine)
	salt and pepper

Salt the salmon steaks and let them sit. Fry the diced pork in a frying pan until it is crisp, and remove it. Add the butter to the pan. Dust the salmon with flour and fry it in the butter until browned on both sides. Pour over the cider, bring to the boil, then reduce heat and simmer until fish is done, about 10 minutes. Season with salt and pepper. Serve garnished with the bacon bits. Serves 4.

TRUCHAS A LA NAVARRA
Trout, Navarre Style

4	large trout (about 350g | 3/4lb each)
150g | 5oz	sliced serrano ham or bacon
	flour
	pinch of crushed thyme
	freshly ground black pepper
	oil

Clean and gut the trout and rub them inside and out with salt. Set aside for 30 minutes. Place a slice of ham in the cavity of each. In a shallow bowl mix the flour with thyme and pepper. Dredge the fish in the flour, shaking off excess. Sauté the trout in enough oil to cover the bottom of the pan, until nicely browned on both sides. Serve with lemon.

CALAMARES EN SU TINTA
Squid in Ink Sauce

1kg | 2lb	small squid
4tbsp	fine breadcrumbs
2	cloves garlic
	flour
4tbsp	oil
1	onion, finely chopped
3	tomatoes, peeled and chopped
100ml | 3 1/2fl oz	white wine
1	bay-leaf
	salt and pepper
	dash of cayenne
	chopped parsley

Clean the squid (see instructions in recipe for fried squid on page 23-24), saving the ink sacs. Place these in a small bowl and add a little wine to cover them. Leave the body pouches whole. Finely chop the wing flaps and tentacles and mix with the breadcrumbs and 1 clove minced garlic. Stuff the squid with this mixture and close them with toothpicks. Dredge in flour, shake off excess and sauté in hot oil until lightly browned. Remove to a casserole. In the same oil sauté the chopped onion and remaining garlic until soft. Add the chopped tomatoes and fry until they begin to give off liquid. Then add the wine, bay-leaf, salt and pepper and cayenne. Cook the sauce for 15 minutes. Crush the ink sacs in the bowl and stir the contents into the sauce. Cook the sauce another 15 minutes. Sieve it if a smooth sauce is desired, then pour over the squid in the casserole. Cover and simmer, or bake in a medium oven, until the squid are very tender, about 25 minutes. If sauce is too thick add a little more liquid. Garnish with chopped parsley and triangles of bread crisp-fried in oil. Serve with white rice on the side. Makes 6 servings.

SHELLFISH

Prawns, crayfish, lobster, crab of several kinds, mussels, scallops, clams and more are favourite fare everywhere in Spain. They are most frequently served as *tapa* or starter, so you will find many suggestions for their preparation in Chapters 1 and 2.

LANGOSTA A LA COSTA BRAVA
Lobster, Costa Brava Style

Langosta refers to the clawless spiny lobster. The clawed lobster, *bogavante,* could be used instead.

2	live lobsters, each about 3/4kg | 1 3/4lb
100ml | 3 1/2fl oz	olive oil
1	onion, finely chopped
1	bay-leaf
1tsp	thyme
1	piece orange peel
1/2tsp	saffron
2	cloves garlic
1tsp	paprika
1	dozen almonds or hazelnuts, blanched, skinned and toasted
1tbsp	parsley
1	slice toasted bread
1tbsp	brandy or dry anise brandy
50g | 2oz	dark chocolate
	dash of cayenne
100ml | 3 1/2fl oz	white wine
	stock as needed

Kill the lobsters by severing the spinal cord with a knife at the back of the head where it joins the body section. Split them open lengthwise, catching all the juices, and remove flesh in large chunks. Discard stomach sac and vein, but save the green tomalley and coral. The shell can be boiled in water to provide stock. Heat the oil in an earthenware or other heat-proof casserole and in it sauté the chopped onion until softened. Add the pieces of lobster and sauté briefly on a high heat with the bay-leaf, thyme and orange peel.

Meanwhile in a blender, make a paste with the saffron, garlic, paprika, toasted almonds, parsley, toasted bread, chocolate, cayenne, brandy and enough white wine to smooth the ingredients. Add the juices from the lobster, "liver" and coral. Pour over the lobster and simmer or bake about 15 minutes. If sauce is too thick, add a little stock. Cooked snails can be added to the casserole with the lobster. Serves 4.

Variation: MAR I TERRA, sea and land, lobster with chicken — a good way of making lobster go further. Use 1 chicken, jointed, and 1 lobster, cut up. After sautéing the lobster, remove it, add the chicken, then the above sauce and cook 20 minutes. Return lobster to the casserole and cook another 15 minutes.

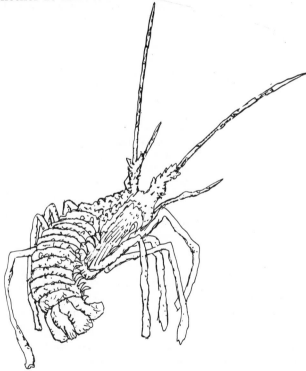

ZARZUELA
Seafood Operetta

A lavish combination of fish and shellfish in a rich sauce, typical of Barcelona and Tarragona.

4	fillets or slices of meaty fish such as angler, conger, dogfish
4	fillets or slices of firm fish such as bass, grouper, bream, gurnard, redfish
4	fillets or slices of flaky fish such as hake, sole, turbot
1/2kg | 1lb	squid, cleaned and cut in rings
1/2kg | 1lb	mussels, scrubbed and steamed open
1/2kg | 1lb	clams, scrubbed and steamed open
8	large prawns, Dublin Bay prawns or lobster
	flour
100ml | 3 1/2fl oz	olive oil
1	onion, finely chopped
3	large tomatoes, peeled and chopped
50ml | 2fl oz	sherry or white wine
2tbsp	brandy or anise brandy
1	bay-leaf
1/2tsp	saffron
2	cloves garlic
6	blanched, skinned and toasted almonds
2	plain biscuits
	salt and pepper
	dash of cayenne
	chopped parsley
	triangles of fried bread
	lemon wedges

Heat some of the oil in a frying pan and slowly sauté the pieces of meaty fish. Remove them to a wide earthenware casserole (or other heat-proof casserole). Continue with the solid-fleshed fish, then the delicate ones, taking care not to overcook them or they will disintegrate. Remove them to the casserole. Dust the squid rings with flour and fry them until browned and put in casserole. Add more oil to the pan and sauté the prawns or crayfish (split lengthwise) or lobster (cut in chunks). Remove and discard empty shells from mussels and clams and put them in the casserole. Save and strain steaming liquid. In the remaining oil sauté the onion until soft. Add the tomatoes and fry for a few minutes. Then add the sherry or wine and the brandy and bay-leaf. In the blender, crush the saffron, garlic, almonds, biscuits, salt, pepper and cayenne, adding a little stock to make a paste. Add this to the tomato sauce with any liquid from mussels and clams. Cook a few minutes, then pour the sauce over the fish and shellfish in the casserole. Shake the casserole to distribute the sauce and continue cooking for about 15 minutes, adding a little additional stock if sauce is too thick. Serve garnished with chopped parsley, fried bread and lemon wedges.

SALT COD

Salt cod *(bacalao)* is enormously popular everywhere in Spain. Before the days of modern, refrigerated transport, it was about the only fish available to people living in the interior of the country. Salt cod should be soaked for 24 hours before cooking, changing the water three or four times.

BACALAO VIZCAINA
Salt Cod, Biscay Style

1kg | 2lb	dry salt cod, soaked
150ml | 1/4pt	olive oil
6	cloves garlic, coarsley chopped
12	dried, sweet red peppers (or substitute 1tbsp
of paprika)	
100g | 3 1/2oz	bacon, diced
2	onions, chopped
1tbsp	chopped parsley
2	tomatoes, peeled and chopped (optional)
	pepper

Soak cod for 24 hours, changing the water 4 or 5 times. After the salt cod has soaked, cut it into large pieces and remove any scales and bones. Pat dry. In an earthenware casserole place the oil and chopped garlic. Heat gently. Add the cod and let it stew in the oil until softened, about 20 minutes.

Drain off the oil and reserve it. Meanwhile, pour boiling water over the dried peppers and let them soak for an hour. Add a spoonful of the reserved oil to an earthenware casserole or frying pan with the diced bacon. Let it fry for a few minutes, then add the chopped onions and parsley. Let them stew very slowly for 30 minutes without allowing them to brown. Remove stems and seeds from peppers, cut them up and add to the onions with a little of their liquid, and tomatoes, if they are being incorporated. Season with pepper. Cook another 30 minutes, adding liquid as needed. Put in blender or processor and process until peppers are finely chopped. Rub the sauce through a sieve and pour it over the cod in the first casserole. Add another spoonful of the reserved oil and a little liquid. Cook slowly (or bake) another 30 minutes, adding more liquid if necessary. The sauce should be thick. Serves 6. As a Lenten dish, the bacon would be omitted.

BACALAO AL PIL PIL
Sizzling Cod

1kg | 2lb	dry salt cod, soaked 24 hours
150ml | 1/4pt	olive oil
8	cloves garlic
1	chilli pepper
2tsp	flour

Cut the soaked cod (see directions in the preceding recipe) crosswise into about 12 pieces. Put it in a pan with water to cover and place on a medium heat until it almost boils. Remove immediately and drain.

Remove any scales and bones, but not the skin. Pat it dry. Put the oil in a flameproof casserole (earthenware is best because it holds the heat). Cut the garlic in thin slivers and add it with the chilli, broken into pieces. Fry until the garlic is lightly toasted and skim out the garlic and chilli and reserve. Put the pieces of cod into the oil in one layer, skin side down and cook for a few minutes, then sprinkle with the flour. Holding the casserole with potholders, swirl it gently from side to side, lifting it off the heat slightly. The gelatinous quality of the skin causes the oil and liquid to emulsify into a sauce the consistency of thick cream. Cook, swirling constantly, for 20 minutes, adding a spoonful of water if sauce becomes too thick. Sprinkle with the reserved garlic and chilli and serve immediately. Makes 6 servings.

VEGETABLES AND SIDE DISHES

PLAIN, BOILED VEGETABLES are practically unknown on Spanish tables, except in restaurants that believe foreigners need a few dull peas and carrots next to their beef steak. Spaniards prefer their veggies either raw in salads, or well-flavoured and well-cooked, often sautéd or stewed in oil with garlic, ham, saffron, herbs, or else simmered in soups, stews and potages (see Main Dishes). Casserole vegetable dishes, sometimes with the addition of eggs, are served as a starter or a main supper entrée.

Vegetarians generally have a terrible time negotiating Spanish menus. It's not that Spaniards eat such a lot of meat. And it's not that there aren't lots of vegetable, grain and pulse dishes. It's that small quantities of meat, ham or sausage are frequently used as flavouring ingredients, so a mess of broad beans, for instance, invariably is stewed with ham; bean or lentil potage with vegetables probably contains sausage, and even a simple side dish of rice could contain some fish.

Vegetables make seasonal appearances at Spanish meals. Springtime brings asparagus *(esparragos),* both cultivated and wild; artichokes *(alcachofas),* broad beans *(habas),* and peas *(guisantes).* Summer means vine-ripened tomatoes *(tomates),* green and red peppers *(pimientos),* cucumber *(pepino),* aubergine or eggplant *(berenjena),* courgette or zucchini *(calabacín),* green beans *(judías verdes).* Autumn into winter brings cabbages *(coles),* cauliflower *(coliflor)* and other members of that family, plus chard *(acelga),* spinach *(espinaca),* and sweet potato *(batata).*

Potatoes have been an important part of the Spanish diet very nearly since Columbus discovered them in America. They are served at just about every meal, as the ubiquitous "chips" to accompany fried steak, fish, or eggs; boiled in the *cocido* with other vegetables; oven-baked in a casserole; puréed with garlic.

Bread, of course, appears at every meal. Spanish bread is wonderful stuff, fresh daily — long, crusty loaves or country-style round ones with a dense crumb. Day-old bread gets toasted and rubbed with oil for breakfast or used to thicken sauces in place of flour, or cubed and fried with ham to accompany eggs.

PISTO
Summer-time Vegetable Dish

Serve this hot or cold. Add chicken, lamb or tuna to the vegetables to create a main dish or top them with a fried egg for a tasty lunch or supper.

50ml | 2fl oz	olive oil
1	large onion, chopped coarsely
2	green peppers, cut in squares
2	cloves garlic, chopped
1	large aubergine
1tsp	salt
	pepper
1tsp	oregano
6	tomatoes, peeled and chopped
1-2	courgettes, sliced or diced

The vegetables may be sliced or cut into large chunks or into fairly small dice; they may be cooked until quite mushy or left very crisp. Heat the oil in a pan or heatproof casserole. In it sauté the onions, green peppers and garlic. Add the aubergine, peeled and cut up, and continue frying until much of the oil has been absorbed. Then season with salt, pepper and oregano and add the prepared tomatoes and courgettes. Cook, covered, on a medium heat until vegetables are tender, about 15 minutes. Remove cover and cook to evaporate liquid. If to be served cold, add a little extra virgin olive oil and a squeeze of lemon to the vegetables immediately before serving. Serves 6.

ESCALIVADA
Catalan Roast Vegetables

450g | 1lb	aubergines
2	red bell peppers
1/2	large onion
1	tomato
1tbsp	extra virgin olive oil
2tbsp	lemon juice
	salt

Cut the aubergines and bell peppers in half. Arrange them, skin side up, on a grill pan with the half onion and tomato. Place under a hot grill until skin is charred and vegetables are tender, about 8 minutes. (Vegetables can also be cooked over hot charcoal — leave them whole and turn to char each side of aubergines and peppers.) Set vegetables aside until cool enough to handle. Peel them and cut flesh into strips. Place all the vegetables in a bowl. Add olive oil, lemon juice and salt to taste. Toss gently. Serve warm, room temperature or cold. Good with roast meat or poultry, grilled sausages, or as a starter.

ALCACHOFAS A LA CORDOBESA
Artichokes, Cordoba Style

12	artichokes (or 1 package frozen artichoke hearts)
	lemon
50ml | 2fl oz	olive oil
3	cloves garlic, chopped
1/2tsp	saffron
1/4tsp	cumin
1tbsp	vinegar
100ml | 3 1/2fl oz	stock or water
1tbsp	flour
1/2kg | 1lb	small new potatoes
1tsp	salt
	sprigs of mint

Trim outer leaves from artichokes, cut off top two-thirds and cut them in half. Rub cut surfaces with lemon and drop into acidulated water. Heat the oil in a casserole and fry the garlic until golden and remove. Crush with the saffron and cumin and mix with the vinegar and stock. Drain the artichokes, add them to the oil and sauté for 5 minutes. Sprinkle with the flour, then add the garlic-saffron liquid. Peel the potatoes, leaving them whole if they are small, or cut them in chunks. Add to the casserole with salt. Cover and cook gently until artichokes and potatoes are tender, about 20 minutes. Garnish with sprigs of mint. Serves 6 to 8.

ALCACHOFAS AL LIMON
Artichokes With Lemon

8-10	artichokes
4tbsp	lemon juice
2	cloves garlic, chopped
3tbsp	olive oil
2tbsp	fine breadcrumbs
100ml ǀ3 1/2fl oz	water
	salt and pepper

Trim off outer leaves of artichokes and cut them in half. Rub them with a little of the lemon juice and put them to cook in boiling salted water. They are done when a leaf pulls off easily, about 15 minutes. Drain well. Meanwhile, in a saucepan or small frying pan sauté the chopped garlic in the oil. Add the breadcrumbs and toast them briefly. Add the lemon juice, the water and salt and pepper and cook for several minutes. Spoon the lemon sauce over the artichoke halves and serve immediately or run under a grill to lightly brown the tops. Serves 8.

CAZUELA DE ESPARRAGOS A LA ANDALUZA
Andalusian Style Asparagus Casserole

1/2kg ǀ 1lb	fresh asparagus or 1 package frozen
50ml ǀ 2fl oz	oil
2	cloves garlic
1	slice bread, crusts removed
1tsp	paprika
1/2tsp	cumin
1tbsp	vinegar
150ml ǀ 1/4pt	water
	salt and pepper
2	eggs

Cut off and discard the woody ends of the asparagus. Chop the stalks into short lengths and blanch them in boiling water for 2 minutes and drain well. Heat the oil in a casserole and fry the garlic and bread until golden. Remove to a blender and crush to a paste with the paprika, cumin, vinegar and some of the water. Add the drained asparagus to the oil and sauté for 5 minutes. Add the garlic paste and remaining water and simmer asparagus until tender, about 15 minutes. The sauce should be thick. Beat the eggs with a little salt and a spoonful of water and pour them over the top of the casserole. Sprinkle with a little paprika and bake in a hot oven until the eggs are set. Serve from the same casserole. Serves 4.

BERENJENAS FRITAS
Fried Aubergine

Peel and slice the aubergines. Layer them in a colander, sprinkling each layer with salt. Let them drain for an hour, then rinse in running water, drain, and pat the slices dry. Dredge them in flour, shaking off excess, and sauté them, a few at a time, in enough olive oil to cover the bottom of the frying pan. Replenish the oil as necessary. Drain on absorbent paper, sprinkle with salt and serve hot.

ESCABECHE DE BERENJENA
Pickled Aubergines

10	tiny aubergines or 6 small ones
150ml | 1/4pt	olive oil
3	cloves garlic, slivered
1	onion, sliced
1	sliced lemon
100ml | 3 1/2 fl oz	vinegar
200ml | 7fl oz	water
1tsp	paprika
1/2tsp	oregano
1tsp	chopped fennel leaves
3tbsp	chopped parsley
1tsp	salt
	freshly ground pepper
1	bay-leaf

If aubergines are very tiny (4cm \| 1 1/2in), pierce them with a knife and leave them whole. Otherwise cut them in half or quarters and pack into a saucepan. Pour over the oil. Add the slivered garlic, sliced onion, lemon, vinegar, water, paprika, oregano, fennel, parsley, salt, pepper and bay. Bring to the boil, reduce heat and cook, covered, until aubergines are tender, 15 minutes. Remove from heat and let them cool in the liquid. Place in jar or other non-reactive vessel, cover and marinate, refrigerated, for at least 3 days before serving. Garnish with fresh, chopped fennel or parsley.

BERENJENAS A LA CATALANA
Catalan Style Aubergines

2	medium aubergines
50ml | 2fl oz	oil
15	hazelnuts
1	onion, chopped
2	cloves garlic, chopped
2	medium tomatoes, peeled and chopped
	salt and pepper
	pinch of cinnamon
	chopped parsley

Peel the aubergines and cut them into cubes. Put them in a colander, salt them and let them sit for an hour. Rinse, drain and pat dry. Heat the oil in a casserole and fry the hazelnuts until toasted and remove them with a skimmer. Add the aubergine to the casserole and sauté it a few minutes. Add the chopped onion and garlic and fry a few minutes, then add the tomatoes. Grind the toasted nuts in a blender and dissolve in a little water or stock. Add to the casserole with salt, pepper and cinnamon. Cook until aubergines are very tender about 15 minutes. Serve sprinkled with chopped parsley.

FAVES AL TOMBET
Alicante Style Broad Beans

800g | 1 3/4lb	shelled broad beans
2	lettuces
4tbsp	oil
1	slice bread
3	cloves garlic
50ml | 2fl oz	water
1tsp	paprika
	salt and pepper

Wash the lettuce and chop it. Heat the oil in a casserole and fry the bread and garlic until golden. Remove them. Add the shelled beans and chopped lettuce to the oil and sauté for several minutes. In the blender crush the bread, garlic, water and paprika. Add to the beans with salt and pepper. Cover and cook slowly until beans are very tender, about 25 minutes, adding more water as necessary. Serves 6.

JUDIAS VERDES SALTEADAS
A LA CASTELLANA
Sautéd Green Beans, Castilian Style

1/2kg | 1lb	green beans
2	red bell peppers
4tbsp	oil or lard
50g | 2oz	ham or bacon, diced
3	cloves garlic
1/2tsp	salt
1tbsp	chopped parsley (or other fresh herbs)
	freshly ground pepper

Snap ends off beans and remove strings if necessary. Put them to cook in boiling salted water until crisp-tender, 8 minutes. Drain. Roast the peppers by spearing them on a fork and holding over gas flame or put them under the grill, turning, until they are blackened and charred on all sides. Cover them with a cloth until cool enough to handle, then peel off all the charred skin. Discard stems and seeds and tear the flesh into strips. Heat the oil in a casserole and sauté the diced ham or bacon with the chopped garlic. Add the beans and the strips of red pepper, parsley, salt and pepper. Toss for several minutes until piping hot. Makes 6 servings.

COLIFLOR AL AJO ARRIERO
Cauliflower, Mule Driver's Style

1	medium cauliflower
75ml | 2 1/2fl oz	oil
4	cloves garlic, chopped
1tsp	paprika
1tsp	salt
1tbsp	vinegar
2tbsp	tomato sauce
2tbsp	parsley, chopped
75ml | 2 1/2fl oz	water

Cut the cauliflower into flowerets. In a frying pan or casserole heat the oil and put in the cauliflower. Sauté gently for 5 minutes, then add the chopped garlic and sauté another few minutes. Add the paprika, salt, vinegar, tomato sauce, parsley and water. Stir well to blend, then cover and cook until cauliflower is tender, about 12 minutes, adding more water as necessary, so a little liquid always remains.

Variation: Prepare potatoes in the same manner.

PIMIENTOS FRITOS
Fried Peppers

16	small, thin green peppers
	salt
150ml | 1/4pt	oil

Wash and dry the peppers. Cut slits in the bottom ends of each and rub a pinch of salt inside each one. Fry them slowly in hot oil, turning to ensure all sides are cooked. They are done when they are quite limp. Drain briefly and serve hot. They can be eaten out of hand or the stems and seeds cut away before serving.

CALABAZA GUISADA
Stewed Pumpkin

1kg | 2lb	pumpkin
2	red or green peppers
1	onion
2	tomatoes

2	cloves garlic, chopped
1/2tsp	cumin
1tsp	salt
1	bay-leaf
4tbsp	oil
200ml	7fl oz	water

Peel the pumpkin and cut it in thin slices. Layer it in a pot or casserole with the peppers, cut in strips, sliced onion, sliced tomatoes. Sprinkle with the chopped garlic, cumin, salt. Add the bay-leaf broken into a few pieces, and drizzle the oil over all. Add the water. Bring the vegetables to a simmer, cover the pot and stew until very tender. Serves 8.

ESPINACAS SALTEADAS
Sautéd Spinach

1 1/2kg	3 1/4lb	spinach
4tbsp	oil
1/2	onion, finely chopped
2	cloves garlic, chopped
1tsp	paprika
1tbsp	vinegar or lemon juice
1/2tsp	salt
1	hard-cooked egg

Wash the spinach in 2 changes of water, trim off stems and cook in a very little water until limp. Drain very well. In a frying pan or casserole heat the oil and fry the chopped onion and garlic. When they are soft, remove pan from heat and add the paprika, vinegar and salt. Add the spinach and return to the heat, tossing it for a few minutes. Add just a little water, cover the pan and simmer for 5 minutes. Serve garnished with sliced egg. The leafy part of chard *(acelga)* can be prepared in the same manner.

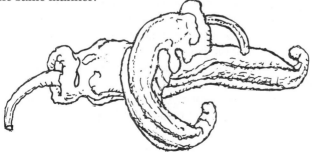

ESPINACAS A LA MALAGUEÑA
Málaga Style Spinach

2kg	4 1/2lb	spinach
3tbsp	oil
3	cloves garlic, chopped
100g	3 1/2oz	Málaga raisins, seeded
50g	2oz	pine-nuts
	pinch of cinnamon
	salt and pepper

Wash the spinach in 2 changes of water, cut off the stem ends and cook in a little water for 5 minutes. Drain. Heat the oil in a frying pan and add the chopped garlic, seeded raisins and pine-nuts. Fry briefly, then add the spinach, chopping it slightly. Mix it well with the raisins and pine-nuts. Season with the cinnamon, salt and pepper and serve hot.

PATATAS A LO POBRE
Poor Man's Potatoes

Possibly the best potato dish in the world.

2kg	4 1/2lb	potatoes
2	onions
150ml	1/4pt	olive oil
1	small green pepper
3	cloves garlic
1/2tsp	ground cumin
1/2tsp	paprika
1tsp	salt
1/2tsp	freshly ground pepper
100ml	3 1/2fl oz	white wine
100ml	3 1/2fl oz	water

Peel the potatoes and slice them fairly thinly. Peel and slice the onions. Pour half the oil into a casserole or heavy frying pan and put in the potatoes, onions and green peppers cut in strips. Pour over the remaining oil. Place on a medium heat, shaking the pan and turning the potatoes with a spatula until they are slightly browned. Crush the garlic with the cumin, paprika, salt and pepper and mix with the wine. Pour over the potatoes with the water. Raise heat to high until liquid is boiling, then reduce to a simmer (or place casserole in a preheated medium oven) and cook without stirring until potatoes are fork-tender, about 30 minutes. Let rest 5-10 minutes before serving. Serves 8.

CACHELOS
Sauced Potatoes

1kg | 2lb	small potatoes
100ml | 3 1/2fl oz	oil
1	onion, chopped
1	clove garlic, crushed
1	bay-leaf
2tsp	paprika
	dash of cayenne
1tbsp	vinegar
	salt to taste

Cut the potatoes in half without peeling them and cook in boiling salted water until fork-tender. Drain very well and set aside. Heat the oil in a frying pan or casserole and sauté the chopped onion until softened. Add the crushed garlic and bay-leaf and stir for a few minutes. Remove from heat and add the paprika and cayenne with the vinegar and a spoonful or more of water. Add the potatoes to the casserole and turn them in the oil for a few minutes. Add salt if necessary, and serve hot. Serves 4-6.

Variation: MOJO COLORADO, Canary Island red sauce. Add ground cumin, oregano and a little water to the above sauce and pour over potatoes, or serve with fish.

PURE DE PATATAS CON AJO
Garlic Potato Purée

1kg | 2lb	potatoes
175ml | 6fl oz	olive oil
2	cloves garlic, crushed
1tsp	salt
	paprika

Peel the potatoes, cut them in pieces and cook in boiling salted water until tender. Drain, saving a little of the water. Mash them or put through a ricer, adding a little of the reserved liquid to make a smooth purée. Mix the oil with the crushed garlic and salt and stir into the potatoes. Serve immediately sprinkled with a little paprika, or reheat in a hot oven. Serves 4-6.

AJO COLORADO
Potatoes Puréed With Garlic
and Red Peppers

Serve as a side dish with meat or chicken or thin and serve, room temperature, spread on bread.

3/4kg | 1 3/4lb	potatoes (3 medium)
1	red bell pepper
2	cloves garlic
1/2tsp	ground cumin
1/2tsp	paprika
1tsp	salt
100ml | 3 1/2fl oz	olive oil
1tbsp	vinegar

Peel the potatoes, cut in quarters. Remove stem and seeds from red pepper. Place them in a saucepan with salted water to cover and boil until potatoes are tender. Drain, saving a little of the liquid. Meanwhile, purée the garlic in a blender with the cumin, paprika, salt, olive oil and vinegar. Remove skin from red pepper and add to the blender. Mash the potatoes or put them through a ricer (blender makes them gummy) and whip in the red pepper mixture until smooth.

MIGAS
Fried Breadcrumbs

A breakfast or supper dish in Spain. Serve it as base for fried eggs, as croutons in soup, as a crunchy addition to green salads or as a side dish instead of chips.

Cut 2-day-old bread into very small dice. Sprinkle with salted water — enough to thoroughly dampen but not soak the bread. Wrap the bread in a dampened tea towel and tie it tightly. Let sit for a few hours or overnight. Heat enough oil or lard to cover the bottom of the frying pan. Fry salt pork or bacon cut in small dice with chopped garlic. Add the bread dice and continue frying, stirring constantly, until toasted. Sprinkle with a little paprika, chopped parsley, salt to taste and, if desired, a little chilli pepper. Garnish with grapes in season or with slices of fried *chorizo* sausage.

EMPEDRADO
"Cobblestones"

250g | 9oz	dried red or black beans, soaked overnight (or a 1/2kg | 1lb tin)
1/2kg | 1lb	rice
100ml | 3 1/2fl oz	oil
1	onion, chopped
3	cloves garlic, chopped
2	tomatoes, peeled and chopped
1litre | 1 3/4pt	water
1tsp	salt
1/4tsp	saffron, crushed

Put the beans to cook in fresh water to cover, adding a bay- leaf and slice of onion, and cook until completely tender. Drain and reserve. In a pot or casserole heat the oil and sauté the chopped onion and garlic. When softened, add the chopped tomatoes and fry 5 minutes. On a high heat add the rice and stir until the grains are opaque. Then add the water, salt and crushed saffron. Bring to the boil, then reduce heat to a simmer and cover. Cook until rice is nearly done, then add the cooked and drained beans and finish cooking. Serves 6-8.

ARROS NEGRE
Black Rice

In Spain, shops which specialize in frozen foods sell tiny sachets of squid's ink. Otherwise, use the ink sacs from three or four squid or cuttlefish (see fried squid recipe on page 23-24 for how to clean squid). The cut up squid or cuttlefish can be added to the rice if desired. The black rice with its seafood flavour is delicious served with baked or grilled white fish or with shellfish.

100ml | 3 1/2fl oz	oil
1	onion, chopped
1	green pepper, chopped
3	cloves garlic, chopped
2	tomatoes, peeled and chopped
900ml | 1 1/2 pt	water or stock
1tsp	salt
4	ink sachets
400g | 14oz	rice

In a pot or casserole heat the oil and sauté the chopped onion, pepper and garlic until softened. Add the chopped tomatoes and continue cooking for 10 minutes. Add the water or stock, salt, and the ink dissolved in a little white wine or stock. Bring to the boil and add the rice. Cover and simmer on a low heat until rice is cooked and liquid absorbed, about 15 minutes. Let sit off the heat for 5 minutes before serving. Serves 4-6.

DESSERTS AND PUDDINGS

SPAIN IS A LAND of fabulous fruit — oranges, apples, pears, peaches, melons, berries, grapes, plus exotic ones such as figs, custard apples, loquats, persimmons, pomegranates... The typical dessert menu is not lengthy. Fresh fruit plus a few puddings and ice-cream are the favoured desserts.

However, Spaniards do love their sweets, and *pastelerías,* pastry shops, are exceedingly popular. Cakes, biscuits, tarts, tortes, buns, sweets and pastries are more usually served between meals, with coffee, tea, cream sherry or sweet Málaga wine, and for holiday meals when certain sweets — such as *turrón* (nougat) at Christmas — are part of the festivities.

Spanish pastries, especially those of Andalusia, are reminiscent of Arabic ones with their eastern spices and flavours — cinnamon, anise, sesame, almond, honey, lemon and orange blossom. Many are not baked, but fried in olive oil.

BIZCOCHO
Sponge Cake

6	eggs
375g | 13oz	sugar
185g | 6 1/2oz	flour, sifted
2tsp	baking powder
1tsp	grated lemon rind

In a large mixing bowl beat the eggs with half the sugar until well combined, then beat for 15 minutes. Mix in remaining sugar, then the flour and baking powder (sifted together), a little at a time, and the grated lemon peel. Butter a sponge cake mould (18cm | 7in) and line with a round of paper, well buttered. Pour in the batter and bake in a preheated medium oven. The cake is done when a knife inserted in the centre comes out clean, about 40 minutes. Let it sit a few minutes, then unmould to cool on a rack. Once cool, the cake can be sprinkled with icing sugar or split horizontally into 2 or 3 layers and filled with fruit or cream filling.

BORRACHOS
Drunken Cakes

1	sponge cake (preceding recipe)
100g | 3 1/2oz	sugar
100ml | 3 1/2fl oz	water
1	piece cinnamon stick
	slivered orange peel
3tbsp	honey
100ml | 3 1/2fl oz	medium sherry or Málaga wine
3tbsp	brandy

Bake the sponge cake in a shallow, rectangular pan. Cut the cooled cake into squares and place them on a platter. Boil the sugar and water with the cinnamon stick, orange peel and honey for 5 minutes. Remove from heat and when partially cooled add the sherry or Málaga wine and the brandy. Spoon this syrup over the squares of cake until all is absorbed. Dust the tops with cinnamon and transfer the squares to a cake platter. Good served with whipped cream.

TORTA DE SANTIAGO
Almond Torte Santiago

450g | 1lb	almonds, blanched and skinned
150g | 50z	butter
1/2kg | 1lb	sugar
7	eggs
150g | 5oz	flour
1	lemon
	icing sugar

Toast the skinned almonds in the oven to bring out their flavour, then grind them finely. Cream the butter with the sugar until fluffy, then beat in the eggs, one at a time. Stir in the flour and the ground almonds. Add the grated rind of the lemon. Put in a buttered, spring-form mould and bake in a moderate oven until a knife inserted in the centre comes out clean, about 1 hour. Cool for 5 minutes, then sprinkle the juice of the lemon over the top. Remove from the mould and cool on a rack. Sprinkle the top with icing sugar (use a template to form the Santiago pilgrims' cross, if desired). Delicious served with tart fruit purée.

ABRAZO DE GITANO
"Gypsy's Embrace" Sponge Roll

This recipe usually appears in cookbooks under the more mundane title of *Brazo de gitano* (Gypsy's Arm).

6	eggs, separated
75g | 2 1/2oz	sugar
75g | 2 1/2oz	flour, sifted
1tsp	grated lemon rind
4tbsp	icing sugar
	custard filling (see following recipe)

Beat the egg whites until stiff. Beat in the yolks one at a time, then the sugar. Add the flour gradually, then the grated lemon rind. Butter a shallow oven tin or sponge-roll pan (about 28x34cm I 11x13in) and line it with well-buttered paper. Pour in the batter and bake in a medium hot oven until the cake is springy, about 10 minutes. While still hot, unmould the cake on to a sheet of paper sprinkled with icing sugar. Remove paper from bottom of cake. Spread cake with the custard filling, reserving a few spoonfuls for the top. With the help of the paper, roll up the cake. Place on a platter, seam-side down, and spread with the remaining custard. Sprinkle with additional icing sugar.

CREMADINA
Custard Filling

225ml | 8fl oz	milk
1	piece cinnamon stick
1	vanilla bean
2tbsp	brandy
2	egg yolks
2tbsp	sugar
1tbsp	flour
	pinch of salt
1tbsp	butter

Place the milk, cinnamon and vanilla bean in a saucepan. Bring to the boil and remove from heat. Stir in the brandy. Put the egg yolks in a bain-marie and whisk them with the sugar, flour and salt until smooth. Place over boiling water and whisk in the hot milk. Cook, stirring constantly, until the sauce begins to thicken. Continue cooking and stirring for 10 minutes. Remove from heat and beat in the butter until custard is smooth and satiny. Cool. Serve as a pudding or a pastry filling.

Variation: Mocha custard filling. Melt 60g | 2oz bittersweet chocolate with the milk and stir in a tablespoon of instant coffee.

GATEAU VASCO
Basque Gâteau

1	recipe *cremadina* custard (above)
200g	7oz	butter
200g	7oz	sugar
2	eggs, separated
300g	10oz	flour
2tsp	baking powder
1tbsp	grated lemon rind
	pinch of salt
50g	2oz	raisins, seeded
2tbsp	brandy

Cream the butter until light and fluffy. Gradually add the sugar, then the 2 egg yolks. Sift together the flour, baking powder and salt. Add to the butter mixture gradually, mixing briefly. Add the grated lemon rind. Form the dough into a ball and let it rest, covered and refrigerated, for 30 minutes. Meanwhile, soak the seeded raisins in brandy. Sprinkle a flan tin or cake mould of about 25cm | 10in with flour. Divide the dough in half. Let it soften slightly at room temperature and roll out one piece on a floured board and fit it into the flan tin. Cover with the prepared custard and sprinkle with the raisins. Roll out the second piece of dough and cover the custard with it. Brush the top with some of the remaining egg white. Use a knife to draw decorative lines on the top. Bake in a preheated hot oven until top is golden, about 30 minutes.

PASTEL CORDOBES
Cordoba Pastry

The filling for this pie, *cabello de angel,* "angel's hair," is confected from a type of squash called *cidra,* which cooks up into golden strands. You could use pumpkin. Cook it, drain well, purée and weigh the pulp. Put in a heavy saucepan with the same weight of sugar plus slivers of lemon peel. Cook very slowly until as thick as a jam. Cool. Or substitute peach jam or orange marmalade.

1/2kg | 1lb	flour
2tsp	salt
100g | 3 1/2oz	lard
200ml | 7fl oz	iced water
1tbsp	vinegar
250g | 9oz	butter
1	egg, beaten
450g | 1lb	"angel's hair" or other fruit preserves
	grated lemon peel
	cinnamon
	sugar

Mix the flour and salt. Cut in the lard, rubbing the mixture through the fingers to combine. Add the iced water and vinegar and combine in a few strokes. Roll into a ball, knead very briefly, and refrigerate the dough, covered, for 30 minutes. Knead the butter until softened. Divide it in half. Place half between sheets of cling film and with a rolling pin spread it to a circle. Roll out second piece of butter in the same manner and refrigerate both, still enclosed in plastic wrap, until chilled. Divide the dough in half. Roll out one half on a floured board. Cover it with a slab of butter. Fold it in thirds, turn and roll out again. Repeat the folding and rolling twice more, then gather into a ball and chill. Repeat with the second piece of dough, layering it with the remaining butter. Chill. Roll out one piece of the dough to line a round or rectangular oven tin. Spread it with the "angel's hair" or preserves. Sprinkle with grated lemon peel. Roll out the remaining dough and fit it over the filling. Roll the edges together to seal. Chill the pastry for 20 minutes. Preheat the oven to very hot. Brush the pastry with beaten egg and bake until golden. Remove and brush again with egg. Sprinkle with sugar and cinnamon and return to oven for a few minutes to dry.

QUESADA
Cheese Custard Tart

A speciality of Cantabria, where it is made with *pasiego,* fresh, unpressed cheese. You could use Spanish *requesón.* Elsewhere use well-drained, natural cottage cheese or Italian ricotta.

1/4litre | 1/2pt	milk
1	piece lemon peel
1	piece cinnamon stick
100g | 3 1/2 oz	fine bread or biscuit crumbs
400g | 14oz	dry cottage cheese
250g | 9oz	sugar
4	eggs
	sugar and ground cinnamon

Put the milk in a pan with the lemon peel and cinnamon stick. Bring to the boil and remove from heat. Beat the cheese in a mixer or with a wooden spoon until smooth. Gradually beat in the sugar, then the eggs, one at a time. Remove lemon peel and cinnamon from milk and mix milk thoroughly with the cheese. Beat in biscuit crumbs. Pour into a shallow baking tin and bake in a medium hot oven until set, about 45 minutes. Test by inserting a knife in the centre; tart is done when it comes out clean. Cool, then unmould. Sprinkle the tart with sugar and cinnamon.

BIENMESABE
Almond Yummies

150g | 50oz	biscuits or wafers
250g | 9oz	almonds, blanched and skinned
1/4litre | 1/2pt	water
250g | 9oz	sugar
1	piece lemon peel
6	eggs
2	egg yolks
	ground cinnamon
	icing sugar

Butter a square tin and line the bottom with a layer of the biscuits. Toast the almonds lightly in the oven, then grind them finely. Place the water, sugar and lemon peel in a heavy saucepan. Bring to the boil and continue boiling until thick. Remove the lemon. Add the ground almonds and stir well. Beat together the eggs and yolks. Stir them into the almond mixture and spread over the layer of biscuits. Bake in a medium oven for 30 minutes. Sprinkle generously with ground cinnamon. When cool, sprinkle with icing sugar and cut into squares.

ENSAIMADAS MALLORQUINAS
Mallorcan Spiral Buns

10g | 1/3oz	pressed yeast
80g | 3oz	sugar
4tbsp	very warm water
1/2kg | 1lb	flour
1tsp	salt
2	eggs
100ml | 3 1/2fl oz	hot water
2tbsp	oil
50g | 2oz	lard or butter
	icing sugar

Dissolve the yeast in 4 tablespoons warm water with 1 teaspoon of the sugar and 100g | 3 1/2oz of the flour. Put in a bowl and cover with a damp cloth and leave to rise in a warm place. In a large bowl mix 400g | 14oz flour, salt, eggs, hot water and remaining sugar. Add the yeast sponge to it. Turn out on to a floured board and knead until very smooth, adding the oil a little at a time and enough additional flour to make a soft, smooth dough. Place the dough in an oiled bowl, turn it to coat evenly and cover with a dampened cloth. Put in a warm place until doubled in bulk, 1 or 2 hours. Melt the lard or butter and let it cool. Punch down the dough and knead it again briefly. Divide it into pieces each of about 40g | 1 1/2oz. Roll each one out quite thinly, brush it with the lard, fold in quarters and roll out and brush again with lard. Then roll the piece of dough into a cord about 25 cm | 10in long. Twist the cord into a spiral, pinching the end underneath so it does not unwind. Place on a lightly greased oven tin. Continue with the remaining pieces of dough, leaving space between them. Cover with a damp cloth and put them in a warm place until they have risen,

THE BEST OF SPANISH COOKING

about 30 minutes. Sprinkle them with cold water and put in a preheated hot oven until golden, 10 to 12 minutes. Remove and sprinkle with icing sugar. Makes about 20 buns.

Variation: Form the dough into 2 very large spirals. After baking, pipe sweetened, whipped cream in the spirals and top with pieces of glacé fruit.

MANTECADOS
Lard Cakes

1/2kg | 1lb	flour
150g | 5oz	almonds, blanched and skinned
250g | 9oz	lard or margarine
200g | 7oz	icing sugar
1/2tsp	cinnamon
1tbsp	sesame seed, toasted
	icing sugar

Spread the flour on an oven tin and toast it in the oven until very lightly coloured, stirring so it toasts evenly. Toast the almonds until golden, then grind them finely. When the flour is cooled, mix with the ground almonds. Beat the lard until it is very creamy. Beat in the sugar and cinnamon, then add the flour-almond mixture a little at a time with the toasted sesame seeds. Roll or pat the dough to a thickness of 1cm | 1/2in. Cut into rounds or squares about 5cm | 2in. Place them on an oven tin. Bake in a slow oven until the cakes are lightly golden, about 30 minutes. Let them cool several minutes before removing from tin. They are fragile. When completely cool, dust with icing sugar. They may be individually wrapped in tissue paper and packed in boxes. Makes about 3 dozen small cakes.

ROSCOS DE VINO
Wine Doughnuts

200ml | 7fl oz	oil
1tbsp	aniseed
2tbsp	sesame seed
100ml | 3 1/2fl oz	Málaga wine
100ml | 3 1/2fl oz	white wine
50ml | 2fl oz	orange juice
1/2kg | 1lb	flour
	icing sugar

Heat the oil in a saucepan with the aniseed and sesame. Cool it. Put it in a bowl with the two kinds of wine and the orange juice. Add enough flour to make a soft dough. Let it rest, covered and refrigerated, at least 2 hours. Roll the dough into thick cords about 8cm | 3in long. Pinch the ends together to form small circles. Place the rings on a lightly oiled baking tin. Let them rest for an hour, then bake in a preheated medium oven about 20 minutes or until lightly coloured. Dredge them in icing sugar while still warm.

ROSCOS
Fried Doughnuts

300ml | 10fl oz	oil
30g | 1oz	aniseed
	grated peel of 1 lemon
700g | 1 1/2lb	sugar
300ml | 10fl oz	milk or orange juice
2tbsp	cinnamon
3	eggs, separated
3tsp	baking soda
1 1/2kg | 3 1/2lb	flour
	oil for deep frying

Put the oil in a saucepan with the aniseed and heat until hot and spice is fragrant. Do not let it burn. Remove and cool the oil. In a large bowl mix the lemon peel with 275g | 9 1/2oz sugar, milk or juice, cinnamon and the cooled oil with aniseed. Add 2 cups of the flour, then beat in the egg yolks and baking soda. Beat the whites until stiff and fold them into the batter. Add flour, using the hands to work it in. At first the dough will be very sticky. Continue adding flour until the dough is just stiff enough to roll without sticking to the hands. Take a small ball of the dough and roll it into a thick cord about 12cm | 4 1/2in long. Pinch the ends together to form a circle. Continue forming the doughnuts. Heat oil, deep enough to cover the doughnuts, until it is very hot but not smoking. Add the rings of dough, a few at a time. Fry until golden brown. Remove with a skimmer, drain briefly and, while still hot, dredge with sugar on both sides. Makes about 10 dozen.

THE BEST OF SPANISH COOKING

BUÑUELOS
Fritters

225ml | 8fl oz	water
70g | 2 1/2oz	butter, margarine, lard or oil
1tbsp	anise brandy (optional)
2tbsp	sugar
1/4tsp	salt
150g | 5oz	flour
3	eggs
	oil for deep frying
	icing sugar

Place the water, butter, anise, sugar and salt in a saucepan and bring the water to the boil. Lower the heat and add the flour all at once, beating it hard with a wooden spoon until it forms a smooth ball of dough. Remove from the heat and beat in the eggs, one at a time. Heat oil, deep enough to cover the fritters, until hot but not smoking. Dip two spoons into oil and use them to form balls of dough and drop them into the oil. The fritters will puff and rise to the surface as they fry. Remove with a skimmer when they are golden. Drain on absorbent paper and sprinkle the fritters with sugar. They may be slit open and filled with custard or jam.

CHURROS
Breakfast Crullers

These are delicious served with thick, hot chocolate for dunking.

1/4litre | 1/2pt	water
50ml | 2fl oz	oil
1/2tsp	salt
200g | 7oz	flour
	oil for deep frying
	sugar

Put the water, oil and salt in a heavy saucepan and bring to the boil. Turn the heat to low and add the flour all at once and beat hard with a wooden spoon until it forms a ball. The batter will be very stiff. Remove from heat. Heat deep oil to almost smoking. Place the dough in icing syringe and pipe strips or rings of the dough into the hot oil, a few at a time. Fry until golden brown. Remove and drain on absorbent paper. Serve immediately sprinkled with sugar. Makes about 30 strips.

CHOCOLATE A LA TAZA
Thick Hot Chocolate

115g | 4oz	dark chocolate, chopped
1litre | 1 3/4pt	milk or water
1tbsp	cornflour
4tbsp	sugar

Place the chocolate and half the milk in a pan and heat, stirring, until the chocolate has melted. Dissolve the cornflour in the remaining milk and whisk into the chocolate with the sugar. Cook on a low heat, whisking constantly, until the chocolate is thickened, about 5 minutes. Remove and whisk smooth. Serve in cups or bowls with *churros*.

TORTITAS DE PLATANO
Banana Pancakes

A speciality of the Canary Islands, Spain's most southerly territory, where bananas thrive.

1/2kg | 1lb	bananas
6	eggs
100ml | 3 1/2fl oz	milk
	pinch of salt
1tsp	cinnamon
	grated rind of 1 lemon
1tsp	baking powder
	pinch of baking soda
130g | 4 1/2oz	flour
2tbsp	brandy
	oil for frying

Peel and mash the bananas. Whisk in the eggs, add milk, salt, cinnamon, lemon rind, and beat well. Sift the baking powder, soda and flour and stir into the banana mixture. Stir in the brandy. (Batter can be mixed in a blender.) Let the batter sit a half-hour. Heat enough oil to cover the bottom of a frying pan. Drop spoonfuls of the batter into the hot oil. Fry until browned on bottom; turn to brown other side. Drain on absorbent paper. Sprinkle with sugar or drizzle with honey which has been boiled with a little water.

RELLENOS DULCES DE CUENCA
Sweet Dumplings, Cuenca Style

300g	10 1/2oz	stale bread
1tbsp	sugar
2	eggs
2tsp	cinnamon
	grating of fresh nutmeg
	pinch of salt
1/2tsp	baking soda
	grated lemon peel
	oil for frying
1	piece cinnamon stick
1	thick slice orange
1	thick slice lemon
200ml	7fl oz	sweet sherry or Málaga wine
125g	4 1/2oz	honey
200ml	7fl oz	water

The bread should be a Spanish, Italian, or French-style loaf without texturizers. Cut into thick slices and put in a bowl. Add water to cover and let the bread soak for 30 minutes. Peel off the softened crust and discard. Squeeze out the water and place the bread in a bowl. Beat it smooth. Add the sugar, eggs, ground cinnamon, nutmeg, salt, baking soda, and grated lemon peel. Heat oil in a frying pan to a depth of 11/2cm l 1/2in. Drop the dumpling mixture by spoonfuls (about the size of a walnut) into the oil and fry until golden. Turn and brown the other side. Remove and drain. In a casserole combine the sherry, honey and water with the cinnamon stick, orange slice and lemon slice. Bring to the boil and cook for 5 minutes. Add the fried dumplings and simmer for 20 minutes. Serve hot or cold. Makes about 20 dumplings.

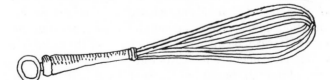

CASADIELLES
Asturian Walnut Rolls

For the pastry dough:

50g | 2oz	lard, butter or margarine
100ml | 3 1/2fl oz	white wine
200g | 7oz	flour
1/4tsp	salt
1/2tsp	aniseed (optional)
	oil for deep frying
	icing sugar

Melt the lard in a saucepan and remove. Add the wine, then beat in enough of the flour with the salt and aniseed to make a smooth dough. Knead very briefly and let it rest, refrigerated, for at least 2 hours.

For the filling:

200g | 7oz	walnuts
100g | 3 1/2oz	sugar
50ml |2fl oz	sherry
100ml | 3 1/2fl oz	water
1	piece cinnamon stick
1	piece lemon peel

Grind the walnuts or chop finely in processor. Make a syrup by boiling for 5 minutes the sugar, sherry, water, cinnamon and lemon peel. Remove the cinnamon and peel and stir in the walnuts. Leave to cool.

Roll out the dough on a floured board and cut squares of about 10cm I 4in. Spread a spoonful of the cooled filling on each square. Fold opposite sides to the centre, overlapping the edges and pinch together. Seal the ends by crimping them with a fork. Heat oil until very hot and fry the rolls, a few at a time, until they are golden. Remove and drain on absorbent paper. Sprinkle with icing sugar.

Variation: Use 2 sheets of frozen puff pastry, thawed, in place of the dough. Place one sheet on a baking tin and spread with the walnut filling. Lay the second sheet on top. Brush with beaten egg and bake in a very hot oven until golden.

ARROPE
Fruit in Wine Syrup

Arrope is fruit soaked in slaked lime and cooked in wine must to preserve it. This is a simple adaptation.

Boil 2litres | 3 1/2pt Málaga wine or grape juice until reduced by half. Add to it the slivered peel of 1 orange and 1 lemon, and 2 dozen dried figs. Simmer for 20 minutes, then add 1kg | 2lb pumpkin, peeled and cut in chunks. Simmer another 15 minutes. Remove from heat. When cool, cover and refrigerate for 24 hours before serving. Dried apricots, prunes and other fruit can be added.

MANZANAS ASADAS AL VINO
Apples Baked With Wine

6	apples
40g | 1 1/2oz	walnuts or almonds, chopped
6tbsp	sugar or honey
	cinnamon
6tsp	butter
300ml | 10fl oz	white wine or cider

Core the apples and put them in a baking dish. Fill the hollows with chopped nuts. Add a spoonful of sugar or honey to each and dust with cinnamon. Top with a teaspoon of butter. Pour in the wine and put the apples in a hot oven until cooked, about 25 minutes. Serve hot or cold.

FLAN AL CARAMELO
Caramel Custard

200g | 7oz	sugar
50ml | 2fl oz	water
3/4litre | 1 1/4pt	milk
	cinnamon stick and lemon peel or vanilla bean
2	egg yolks
3	whole eggs

Put 115g | 4oz of the sugar in a heavy saucepan with the water. Cook on a low heat until the sugar is dissolved, then boil without stirring until the sugar turns a golden caramel colour.

Remove immediately and pour into 6 prepared custard moulds. Tilt them to coat the bottoms with the caramel. Reserve. Place the milk, cinnamon and lemon or vanilla bean in a pan and heat to boiling and remove. Whisk together the yolks and eggs and add the remaining 85g | 3oz sugar. Whisk the hot milk into the egg mixture. Pour the custard through a sieve into the prepared moulds. Place them in an oven pan and add hot water to half their depth. Put in a preheated medium oven until the custards are set, about 45 minutes. Cool the custards and chill them. Unmould on to serving plates.

CREMA CATALANA
Catalan Custard With Burnt Sugar Topping

6	egg yolks
200g | 7oz	sugar
3/4litre | 1 1/4pt	milk
1	piece cinnamon stick
1	piece lemon peel
3tbsp	cornflour

Beat the egg yolks in a bowl until light. Whisk in 150g | 5oz of the sugar. Put the milk in a saucepan with the cinnamon stick and lemon peel. Bring to the boil and remove from heat. Strain it through a sieve and whisk into the egg mixture. Dissolve the cornflour in a few tablespoons of milk or water and whisk into the custard. Return the custard to the saucepan and place over a low heat. Cook, stirring constantly, until it just begins to bubble. Remove and place in a shallow pudding bowl or in 6 individual heat-proof plates. Let the custard cool, then chill. Before serving, sprinkle the custard with the remaining sugar. Caramelize it with a hot salamander (improvise with a metal spatula or small grid heated red-hot) or place the custards under a hot grill until sugar has melted. Serve with rosettes of whipped cream and crisp biscuits.

TOCINO DEL CIELO
"Heavenly" Custard Squares

250g | 9oz	sugar
300ml | 1/2pt	water
1	piece lemon peel
8	egg yolks
1	whole egg

Place 150g | 5oz sugar in a heavy saucepan with 4 tablespoons water. Cook on a low heat until sugar is dissolved then boil until a caramel colour. Remove immediately from heat and pour into a heat-proof tin or pudding mould, about 14cm | 5 1/2in square, tilting to coat the bottom. Put the remaining sugar and water in saucepan with the lemon peel. Bring to the boil and cook the syrup to the thread stage (forms a thread of syrup when dropped from a spoon). Beat the egg yolks and whole egg until combined, then beat in the hot syrup. Strain the custard into the caramel-lined mould. Cover tightly with foil. Set the mould on a trivet or rack in a larger pan and add boiling water to the pan. Cover tightly and steam the custard (or place in fairly hot oven) until a knife inserted comes out clean, about 20 minutes. Remove from heat and let cool completely. Run a knife around the edge of the custard and unmould it on to a serving dish. Cut the custard into small squares.

NATILLAS
Creamy Custards

1/2litre | 1pt	milk
1	piece cinnamon stick
1	piece lemon peel
1	vanilla pod
4	egg yolks
100g | 3 1/2oz	sugar
1tbsp	cornflour
3tbsp	milk
	biscuits or ladyfingers
	ground cinnamon

Place the milk, cinnamon, lemon peel and vanilla in a sauce-pan and bring to the boil. Remove from heat and strain. In a saucepan or bain-marie beat the egg yolks with the sugar until they are thick and pale. Whisking the yolks, pour in the hot milk. Dissolve the cornflour in the 3 tablespoons milk and whisk into the custard. Set the pan over boiling water and cook, stirring, until the custard is thickened, about 10 minutes. It should be thick enough to coat a spoon. Remove from heat and cool. Place biscuits or ladyfingers in four pudding bowls and divide the custard among them. Sprinkle generously with cinnamon, and chill. The custard will be the consistency of very thick cream. If desired, the egg whites can be whipped with sugar to make a meringue. Either bake on an oven tin or spread over the puddings and place in hot oven until meringue is browned, then cool.

LECHE FRITA
"Fried Milk"

150g | 5oz	butter
250g | 9oz	flour, sifted
150g | 5oz	sugar
1/2litre | 1pt	milk
1	piece cinnamon stick
1	piece lemon peel
4	eggs, separated
125g | 4oz	fine breadcrumbs
	oil for frying
	sugar

In a heavy saucepan melt the butter and add 175g | 6oz sifted flour. Stir and let cook gently. Then add the sugar. Scald the milk with the cinnamon and lemon peel. Strain it and add to the butter mixture, stirring constantly as it thickens. When it starts to bubble, remove from heat and add the egg yolks, one by one, incorporating each before adding the next. Lightly oil a rectangular tin or dish and spread the mixture in it to a thickness of about 2cm | 3/4in. Chill in the refrigerator until set, at least 2 hours. Cut the batter into squares or triangles of about 5cm | 2in. Dip each into flour, then into lightly beaten egg white, then breadcrumbs. Fry in hot oil, turning to brown on both sides. Sprinkle with sugar. Serve hot or cold. Makes about 2 dozen.

ARROZ CON LECHE
Creamy Rice Pudding

250g | 9oz	medium short-grain rice
1/4litre | 1/2pt	water
1	piece cinnamon stick
1	piece lemon peel
75g | 2 1/2oz	sugar
1/4tsp	salt
1 1/4litres | 2 1/4p t	milk
	ground cinnamon

Put the rice, water, cinnamon stick and lemon peel in a saucepan and bring to the boil. Cover and simmer on a low heat until the water is nearly absorbed, about 8 minutes. Then add the sugar, salt and milk and continue cooking until the rice is very tender. There should be enough liquid left to give the pudding a creamy consistency. Remove cinnamon and lemon rind. Serve chilled, dusted thickly with ground cinnamon.

LECHE MERENGADA
Iced Meringue Milk

1litre | 1 3/4pt	milk
1	cinnamon stick
1	piece lemon peel
175g | 6oz	sugar
3	egg whites
	ground cinnamon

Put the milk, cinnamon stick, lemon peel and all but 3 tablespoons of the sugar in a saucepan and bring to the boil. Reduce heat and simmer for 15 minutes. Remove cinnamon and lemon. Whip the egg whites until stiff, beating in the reserved 3 tablespoons of sugar. Beating constantly, slowly add the hot milk. Serve chilled or freeze the mixture until it is slushy, then put in blender or mixer and beat and freeze again (or freeze in a sorbet machine).

HELADO DE CANELA
Cinnamon Ice-Cream

1/4litre | 1/2pt	milk
1	cinnamon stick
1	piece lemon peel
300g | 10oz	sugar
8	egg yolks
	pinch of salt
1tbsp	ground cinnamon
1/2litre | 1pt	cream

Put the milk, cinnamon stick, lemon peel and sugar in a saucepan. Bring to the boil, lower heat and cook 15 minutes. Strain. Beat the egg yolks with the salt until they are thick and pale. Put in a bain-marie over boiling water and cook, stirring, until they thicken. Then whisk in the milk and continue cooking until thick enough to coat a spoon. Remove from heat and continue whisking until the mixture is creamy and cooled. Beat in the cream and chill the mixture. Freeze in ice-cream maker, or freeze, beat in blender or mixer, and freeze again.

GASTRONOMIC SOUVENIRS FROM SPAIN

SPANISH MARKETS and supermarkets are a great place to shop for souvenirs. Spanish foods make fine gifts for friends back home and will inspire you to experiment with typical dishes in your own kitchen.

If travelling outside EEC countries, check customs regulations. Some countries prohibit the entry of meats, dairy products and unprocessed fruits and vegetables.

Saffron and other spices and herbs. Almost as precious as gold, saffron *(azafrán)* will please your gourmet friends and make your own paella authentic. Grown extensively in La Mancha and Murcia, it is much less expensive in Spain than abroad. It comes in wispy threads of deep orange which are the whole, dried stigmas of the saffron crocus. They are usually packaged in tiny plastic boxes, from a half to two or more grams. Half a gram is enough for two sizeable paellas, two pots of bouillabaisse or three batches of risotto Milanese.

Large markets have stalls specializing in spices and herbs where you can buy them whole and ground, by weight. Other good buys are bags of whole nutmeg *(nuez moscada)*, cinnamon sticks *(canela)*, aniseed *(matalahuga)* and cumin *(comino)*. If you've enjoyed Spanish or Moroccan *pinchitos,* spicy meat kebabs, be sure to purchase some *especia para pinchitos,* a Moroccan-style spice blend which is used to marinate the meat. Check the spice stalls and herbalists too for a selection of herbal teas.

Dried fruits and nuts. Figs, raisins and almonds are some of Spain's finest produce. Figs grow everywhere in southern Spain, the tree as much a part of the landscape as the olive. Figs *(higos)* ripen in late summer and are dried and pressed. They are often marketed in woven baskets. They are used to confect *pan de higos,* a spicy, sweet fig roll studded with almonds, which can be found in shops around Christmas time.

Raisins *(uvas pasas)* are dried muscatel grapes, the plumpest and sweetest of raisins. They come prettily packaged and are found in supermarkets everywhere.

Spain is the world's second producer of almonds *(almendras).* Buy them shelled or unshelled. Purchased from open stock, rather than packaged, they are cheaper. Other good buys are those pricey pine-nuts *(piñones)* and hazelnuts *(avellanas).*

Olives. Spanish olives are world famous. Best known are the fat, Seville *manzanillas,* which are widely exported. On their home ground, olives come in many more varieties. Try gourmet olives stuffed with anchovies, almonds, pimento or onions and home-cured ones redolent of herbs and garlic, tangy with vinegar, red with paprika or zingy with chilli pepper. Supermarkets sell olives bottled, tinned and sealed in plastic envelopes. Some have stands where olives are dipped from barrels and weighed out. If you buy olives from open stock to take back home, drain off all the liquid by placing them in a colander. Then seal in plastic bags and put in plastic containers (so they don't leak in your suitcase). When you get them home, put in jars and cover with a strong brine (salt water). Refrigerate and they will keep for many months. Though you'll probably find your friends will devour them long before.

Olive oil. Olive oil has attained gourmet status in international cuisine and, though supermarkets abroad often have a good selection, the prices are better in Spain. Spain produces more olive oil than any other country in the world. Much of it is exported, bottled and distributed by other countries under their own labels.

Olive oil is marketed in two types. *Aceite de oliva* is a mixture of refined and virgin olive oil. It is fairly mild in flavour, without the fruitiness so prized in virgin oil. *Extra virgen* is "olive juice," first pressing, unrefined. It is much more expensive. A few extra virgin oils are allowed *denominación de origen* or place-of-origin labels. Look for Borjas-Blancas of Lérida, Siurana of Tarragona, Sierra de Segura of Jaén and Baena of Córdoba.

Capers. Capers *(alcaparras)* are the pickled flower-buds of the caper bush and gourmet cooks love them. Spain is the world's biggest producer of capers and they are less expensive here than abroad. The tiny ones are the most appreciated and costly.

Tinned foods. Friends abroad are always delighted to receive a little "taste of Spain." Try them on something a little unusual, like squid in its own ink or octopus in tomato sauce; or choose pickled mussels, tuna or bonito in sauce, brined cockles, sardines in piquant sauce. Besides seafood, other tinned foods are tiny, pickled aubergines *(berenjenas de Almagro); fabada,* possibly the best tinned beans in the world; *pisto,* which is similar to ratatouille; white asparagus from Aranjuez.

Vinegar. Sherry vinegar made from real sherry from Jerez is deservedly famous and much favoured by nouvelle chefs. Also excellent is Montilla wine vinegar, which is not as pricey as sherry vinegar. You may have to search out these gourmet vinegars.

Conserves and preserves. It wouldn't be proper English marmalade without the wonderfully aromatic, bitter oranges of Spain. Though marmalade is by no means an exclusively Spanish product, the prices here are very good. Taste two or three brands. Another gastronomic treat is *dulce de membrillo,* quince jelly. This is sold in large tins, from which squares are cut and weighed, or in sealed, plastic packets. In a covered container it will keep for a long time. Serve quince jelly as a sweet course accompanied by a slice of white cheese and a few almonds or walnuts.

Rice. Medium short-grain rice, essential for paella making, is not always easy to find back home where long-grain pilaff rice is preferred. Buy real Spanish rice.

Garlic. In tourist areas vendors peddle garlands of garlic in the streets. One wonders whether the tourists who carry them back to Britain actually use the pungent buds in cooking or just hang them on the kitchen wall to look rustic. In any case, they are inexpensive and make fine gifts. You will also find *ajetes,* tender garlic shoots, fresh and bottled.

If you're the recipient of a gift of garlic, keep it in a cool, dry, well-ventilated spot away from direct sunlight. Don't refrigerate garlic bulbs.

Cheeses. Spanish cheeses deserve more publicity than they get, for there are some excellent ones. Manchego is the best known. A ewes' milk cheese from central Spain, it is marketed semi-cured and aged. Aged Manchego is splintery like Parmesan with a tantalizing bite to it. Some other good ones: Cabrales, a blue cheese made of cows' milk, creamy, sharper than Roquefort; Gallego, a pale yellow, mild cows' milk cheese; Idiazabal, a smoked and cured ewes' milk cheese, smooth and pungent; Roncal, sharp but mellow; San Simon, a cows' milk cheese with a mild, smoky flavour; Burgos and Villalón, fresh, white cheeses, good with fruit or as a dessert, drizzled with honey. The last two shouldn't be too long out of the refrigerator, so purchase them only if your travel time is no more than a few hours.

Charcuterie. A whole Spanish *serrano* ham will flavour your memories of Spain for quite a long time. Cost is a good index of quality, and those with "surnames" indicating origin are the priciest. Particularly appreciated are those of Jabugo (Huelva) made from the black Iberian pig *(pata negra),* Montanchez (Cáceres), Trevélez (Granada), Lérida and Teruel. If you're buying a whole ham, look for the metal stamp, the producer's guarantee. These hams are served raw, sliced very thinly immediately before serving. Supermarkets sell industrially-produced *"serrano"* hams, bone removed, which are machine-sliced. Keep tightly wrapped and consume within a few days as the sliced ham dries out quickly.

Spain produces some very distinctive sausages. Try *chorizo,* spiked with garlic and coloured red with strong paprika; *butifarra,* Catalan white (or black) pork sausage; *sobrasada,* Mallorcan soft sausage to spread on toasted slabs of bread; *morcilla,* black pudding with rice, pine-nuts, cloves, aniseed and cinnamon, and *longaniza,* thin, hard sausage.

Pastries and sweets. Visitors to Spain are tempted by the aroma of sugared-coated almonds, *garapiñadas,* confected by street vendors who proffer free samples. They are wonderfully addictive. Buy quantities of them to take back for friends.

Another famous almond candy is *turrón,* nougat, which can be found in food shops and at open-air sweet stalls at village fairs. *Turrón* and *mazapan,* almond marzipan candies, are both traditional Christmas fare. The Christmas holiday season brings other packaged sweets to supermarkets. Look for *roscos, mantecados,* and *polvorones.* They are sugared, spice-flavoured biscuits.

Wines and liqueurs. Spain produces some of the world's best wines. Their prices in Spain are often only half those charged on the shelves in London.

Most Spanish wines bear a label designating the region of origin — *denominación de origen.* Certainly the best-known of these are Rioja for red and white table wines, and Jerez for sherry. Catalonia produces the best *cava,* which is Spanish for sparkling wine made by the *"methode champenoise."* Málaga wine is liquid raisins — a lovely after-dinner tipple.

Anise-flavoured distilled liqueur, dry or sweet, is *aguardiente de anís.* Spanish workers drink it for breakfast, sometimes in a cup of tea; Spanish ladies drink it instead of afternoon tea. *Pacharán* is a Navarre digestive, flavoured with anise and sloe-berries. Serve it over ice. Most Spanish brandy comes from the sherry bodegas in Jerez. Many well-known liqueurs are produced in Spain and are cheaper than in other countries, so do some comparison shopping for your favourites.

Cookware. Cooks just love receiving kitchenware and cooking utensils. Earthenware casseroles and terrines, though heavy, make wonderful gifts. Look around, also, for wood or brass mortar and pestle, paella pans, pinchito skewers, olive wood bowls, oil and vinegar cruets, wooden olive dippers, colourful pitchers for *sangría.* Shop antique stores for decorative ceramic tiles and dishes.

GLOSSARY OF INGREDIENTS

OUTSIDE SPAIN, most ingredients for Spanish cooking will be found at your supermarket. You might have to search for a few items in Spanish or Caribbean food shops.

Aceite, aceite de oliva: oil, olive oil. For authentic flavour, use olive oil when recipes in this book call for oil. The very finest olive oil is labelled "extra virgin." That labelled "pure olive oil" is refined olive oil to which a little virgin oil is added for flavour. You may substitute other vegetable oils if preferred, but do not combine olive oil and vegetable oil for frying. Do not use butter or margarine in place of oil in Spanish cookery.

Aguardiente: any distilled liquor, but particularly anise brandy, either dry or sweet. Similar in flavour are Sambucco or Pernod. In Galicia, *aguardiente* is a clear grape brandy, similar to French *marc* or Italian *grappa.*

Azafrán: saffron. Spice with distinctive yellow colour and flavour, essential for paella and many other Spanish dishes. To use it, crush the threads to a powder in a mortar, or in a teacup with the butt-end of a knife (easier to crush if toasted lightly in a dry pan). Add a little water, stock or wine to dissolve the saffron and let it sit for 10 minutes before incorporating in rice, soup or sauce. If saffron is not available, use yellow food colouring. Do not substitute turmeric, which has its own very different flavour.

Beicon, panceta, tocino: bacon, salt pork. Salt belly pork is much used in Spanish stews and potages. You could substitute unsmoked, streaky bacon. For cooking, it should not be cut in rashers, but left in a slab.

Butifarra: Catalan sausage, white and black. Substitute a light sausage such as bratwurst for the white; black pudding for the black.

Cazuela de barro: earthenware casserole. These are much used in Spain, for cooking and for serving. Clay casseroles can be used directly on gas flames but should have a diffuser if placed on an electric hob. Bring up to heat gently; never place directly on a high heat nor put a hot casserole on a cold surface. Clay casseroles are excellent for oven cookery. They hold heat quite a long time, so food continues to cook after being removed from the oven. Soak new earthenware utensils in water to cover for several hours before first use. Do not store acid foods in earthenware.

Chorizo: pork sausage, highly-flavoured with garlic and paprika. Hard-cured varieties are served sliced with bread. Soft ones, usually tied in short links, are fried or added to stewed beans and lentils.

Fabes: big, white, dried beans. Essential for Asturian *fabada.* If not available, use dried lima beans or butter beans.

Jamón serrano: salt-cured raw ham. Served, sliced thinly, as an aperitif with sherry. Used in cooking for flavour. If not available, substitute Italian Parma (prosciutto) or German Westphalian ham. In cooking unsmoked gammon or lean bacon can be substituted for Spanish ham.

Manteca: Lard. Rendered pork fat — lard — is used in many dishes. Substitute oil in cooked dishes, or butter or margarine in pastry-making.

Morcilla: blood sausage. Made with rice, cinnamon, pepper, anise, sometimes pine-nuts. Some are smoked. If Spanish *morcilla* is not available, use any black pudding.

Pacharán: dry anise brandy flavoured with sloe-berries. Typical of the Basque region and Navarre. Served over ice as a digestive. Also useful in cooking and marinating.

Legumbres secas: pulses. Dry, white haricot beans, *alubias* or *habichuelas,* and chick-peas, *garbanzos,* are the most usual. All should be soaked overnight and drained before being put to cook. Lentils, *lentejas,* don't need soaking.

Vinagre. Use any wine vinegar

Vino. Wine in cooking — red, white and sherry — is dry unless otherwise specified.

CONVERSION CHARTS

NOTE FOR AMERICAN READERS: The recipes in this book are given in Metric and British measurements. We suggest you buy an inexpensive two-kilo set of scales and a one-litre measuring cup. It's much simpler than trying to convert metric recipes into familiar measures.

Following is a table of *approximate* equivalents of commonly used foods (based on ingredients in Spain).

	American Standard Measure	Avdp. Weight	Metric Weight
Butter, margarine	1 tbsp	1/3 oz	13 g
	7 1/2 tbsp	3 1/2 oz	100 g
	1/2 cup	3 2/3 oz	105 g
Cheese, grated	3/4 cup	3 1/2 oz	100 g
Cornflour	1 tsp		3 g (5 ml)
	1 tbsp	1/3 oz	10 g (15 ml)
Flour (all purpose)	3/4 cup	3 1/2 oz	100 g
	1/4 cup	1 1/4 oz	35 g
	1/2 cup	2 1/4 oz	65 g
	1 cup	4 1/2 oz	130 g
	3 3/4 cups	1 lb 2 oz	500 g
Gelatin	1 tbsp	1/4 oz	7 g
Rice	1 cup	7 oz	200 g
Salt	1 tbsp	1/2 oz	15 g
Sugar (granulated)	1 tbsp	1/2 oz	15 g
	1/4 cup	2 oz	55 g
	9 tbsp	3 1/2 oz	100 g
	1 cup	6 oz	175 g

The following chart lists some (very approximate) equivalents.

Food	Quantity	Weight
Almonds, other nuts	40	50 grams
Breadcrumbs	8 tbsp (1/2 cup)	50 grams
Capers	4 tbsp	50 grams
Mussels	2 1/2 dozen	1 kilo
Olives	20 (pitted or stuffed)	50 grams
Onion	1 medium	150 grams
Peas	1 1/2 cups shelled	1/2 kilo
Potatoes	7-8 medium	1 kilo
Tomatoes	4 large	1 kilo
Tomato sauce	2 tbsp	30 ml

FLUID MEASURES
METRIC/BRITISH STANDARD

10 MILLILITRES = 1/3 OUNCE
50 MILLILITRES = 1 3/4 OUNCES
100 MILLILITRES = 3 1/2 OUNCES
250 MILLILITRES = 8 1/2 OUNCES
500 MILLILITRES = 17 1/2 OUNCES
1 LITRE = 1 3/4 PINTS

1 TEASPOON = 5 MILLILITRES
1 TABLESPOON = 18 MILLILITRES
1 OUNCE = 28 MILLILITRES
1 PINT = 570 MILLILITRES
1 QUART = 1.14 LITRES
1 GALLON = 4 1/2 LITRES

FLUID MEASURES
METRIC/U.S. STANDARD

10 MILLILITRES = 2 TEASPOONS
50 MILLILITRES = 3 TABLESPOONS
100 MILLILITRES = 3 1/2 OUNCES
250 MILLILITRES = 1 CUP + 1 TABLESPOON
500 MILLILITRES = 1 PINT + 2 TABLESPOONS
1 LITRE = 1 QUART + 3 TABLESPOONS

1 TEASPOON = 5 MILLILITRES
1 TABLESPOON = 15 MILLILITRES
1 OUNCE = 30 MILLILITRES
1 CUP = 235 MILLILITRES
1 PINT = 475 MILLILITRES
1 QUART = 950 MILLILITRES
1 GALLON = 3 3/4 LITRES

OVEN TEMPERATURE

TEMPERATURE	DIAL NUMBER
VERY SLOW = 250F/120C	= 1/4
SLOW = 300F/150C	= 1
MODERATE = 350F/180C	= 4
HOT = 400F/200C	= 6
VERY HOT = 450F/230C	= 8

WEIGHT
METRIC/OUNCES & POUNDS

10 GRAMS = 1/3 OUNCE	1/2 OUNCE = 14 GRAMS
50 GRAMS = 1 3/4 OUNCES	1 OUNCE = 28 GRAMS
100 GRAMS = 3 1/2 OUNCES	1/4 POUND = 110 GRAMS
250 GRAMS = 8 3/4 OUNCES	1/2 POUND = 230 GRAMS
500 GRAMS = 1 POUND + 1 1/2 OUNCES	1 POUND = 450 GRAMS
1 KILO = 2 POUNDS + 3 1/4 OUNCES	

LINEAR MEASURES
METRIC/INCHES & FEET

1 MILLIMETRE = 1/25 INCH	1/5 INCH = 5 MILLIMETRES
1 CENTIMETRE = 2/5 INCH	1/4 INCH = 6.2 MILLIMETRES
10 CENTIMETRES = 3 9/10 INCHES	1 INCH = 2 1/5 CENTIMETRES
1 METRE = 3 FEET 4 4/5 INCHES	1 FOOT = 30 CENTIMETRES

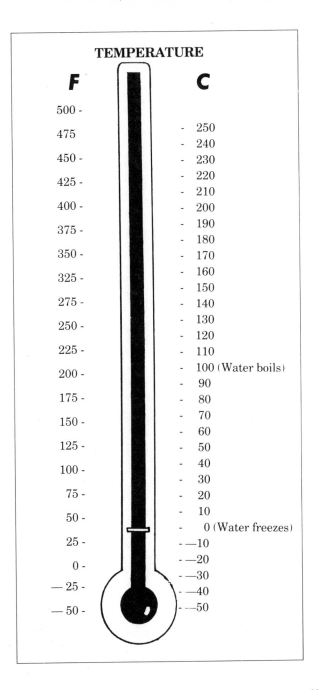

TEMPERATURE

F	C
500 -	
475	- 250
	- 240
450 -	- 230
425 -	- 220
	- 210
400 -	- 200
	- 190
375 -	- 180
350 -	- 170
	- 160
325 -	- 150
275 -	- 140
	- 130
250 -	- 120
225 -	- 110
	- 100 (Water boils)
200 -	- 90
175 -	- 80
	- 70
150 -	- 60
125 -	- 50
	- 40
100 -	- 30
75 -	- 20
	- 10
50 -	- 0 (Water freezes)
25 -	- —10
	- —20
0 -	- —30
— 25 -	- —40
— 50 -	- —50

INDEX OF RECIPES

400 Great Spanish Recipes!

Cooking in Spain, by Janet Mendel, is the definitive guide to Spanish cuisine, with more than 400 great Spanish recipes. Plus complete information on Spain's regional specialities and culinary history, how to buy the best at the market, a complete English-Spanish glossary with more than 500 culinary terms, handy conversion guide... all of it illustrated with colour photographs.

"...A brilliant guide to traditional Spanish cooking. The food is both authentic and accessible, with excellent introductions..."
—*Taste Magazine, Great Britain*

"...Whether you live in the United States, Germany, Iceland or Bahrain, I'm sure you'll find **Cooking in Spain** as fascinating as I did..."
—*Stars and Stripes, Germany*

"...A great source for tapa recipes, and those wonderful vegetable-and-seafood-rich dishes that distinguish the Spanish table..."
—*San Francisco Examiner, USA*

"...Janet Mendel brings the flavour of Spain to your kitchen..."
—*The Gibraltar Chronicle, Gibraltar*

On sale at bookstores in Spain, or by post from
Ediciones Santana S.L., Apartado 422
29640 Fuengirola (Málaga) Spain

More Great Books
from Spain

Birds of Iberia *by Clive Finlayson and David Tomlinson.*
240 pages (Hardback, large format)
A journey through the different regions of this fascinating
peninsula which describes the main habitats and birds found there,
migration patterns and ornithological sites. Beautifully illustrated
throughout with fine line drawings and more than 150 colour
photographs, the book is an appreciation of the extraordinarily
rich and varied birdlife.

Expand Your Spanish *by Linda Hall de Gonzalez. 240 pages*
Tackle the dreaded Spanish subjunctive and chuckle at the same
time? You can with this book. The author keeps you smiling as
she leads you through the minefield of Spanish grammar. Not a
language book in the conventional sense, but it will help you over
the obstacles that put many people off learning the language.

A Selection of Wildflowers of Southern Spain *by Betty
Molesworth Allen. 260 pages*
Southern Spain is host to a rich variety of wildflowers in widely
diverse habitats, some species growing nowhere else. This book
describes more than 200 common plants of the region, each
illustrated in full colour with simple text for easy identification
and enjoyment.

Inside Andalusia *by David Baird. 187 pages*
A travel adventure through Spain's most fascinating region. David
Baird invites you to explore an Andalusia you never dreamt of, to
meet its people, and discover its exciting fiestas. Illustrated with
brilliant colour photographs.

Spanish Property Owners' Community Handbook
by David Searl. 100 pages
Do you know your rights and obligations as a member of your
community of property owners? Here, at last, are the answers!
Including full text, in Spanish and English, of the *Ley de la
propiedad horizontal,* with comments by legal writer David Searl.

The Story of Spain *by Mark Williams. 272 pages*
The bold and dramatic history of Spain, from the caves of Altamira to our day. This is a story of kings and poets, saints and conquistadores, of Torquemada, Picasso, Cervantes, Franco, the Alhambra, the Escorial... Mark Williams has drawn on years of rigorous research to re-create the drama, excitement and pathos of crucial events in the history of the western world. Illustrated in colour.

Gardening in Spain *by Marcelle Pitt. 212 pages*
Your most valuable tool for successful gardening in Spain. How to plan your garden, what to plant, when and how to plant it, how to make the most of flowers, trees, shrubs, herbs. Illustrated with full-colour photographs.

Cooking in Spain *by Janet Mendel. 380 pages*
The definitive guide to cooking in Spain, with more than 400 great Spanish recipes. Plus complete information on Spain's regional specialities and culinary history, how to buy the best at the market, a complete English-Spanish glossary with more than 500 culinary terms, handy conversion guide... all of it illustrated with colour photographs.

You and the Law in Spain *by David Searl. 210 pages*
Thousands of readers have relied on the best-selling You and the Law in Spain to guide them through the Spanish legal jungle. Now, author David Searl brings you a new, completely revised edition with even more information on taxes, work permits, cars, banking in Spain, buying property, Spain and the European Community, and lots more. It's a book no foreigner in Spain can afford to be without.

Excursions in Southern Spain *by David Baird. 280 pages*
40 great trips through Andalusia, from the premier travel writer in Spain today. Here, at last, is a handy guided tour of Spain's most fascinating region, packed with practical information, interesting facts, tips on where to eat and where to stay, and clear maps.

On sale at bookstores in Spain, or by post from
Ediciones Santana, S.L., Apartado 422,
29640 Fuengirola (Málaga), Spain